Money

Editor: Tracy Biram

Volume 391

independence
educational publishers

First published by Independence Educational Publishers

The Studio, High Green

Great Shelford

Cambridge CB22 5EG

England

© Independence 2021

ISBN-13: 978 1 86168 849 1

Printed in Great Britain

Zenith Print Group

Contents

Introduction

Money is Volume 391 in the **issues** series. The aim of the series is to offer current, diverse information about important issues in our world, from a UK perspective.

ABOUT MONEY

Money plays a huge role in our lives, in our society and in the wider world. This book explores the function of money and banks, money management, debt, and the importance of financial education for young people. It considers the future of money, looking at developments like bitcoin and the rise of cryptocurrencies and also the possibility of moving towards a cashless economy.

OUR SOURCES

Titles in the **issues** series are designed to function as educational resource books, providing a balanced overview of a specific subject.

The information in our books is comprised of facts, articles and opinions from many different sources, including:

♦ Newspaper reports and opinion pieces

♦ Website factsheets

♦ Magazine and journal articles

♦ Statistics and surveys

♦ Government reports

♦ Literature from special interest groups.

A NOTE ON CRITICAL EVALUATION

Because the information reprinted here is from a number of different sources, readers should bear in mind the origin of the text and whether the source is likely to have a particular bias when presenting information (or when conducting their research). It is hoped that, as you read about the many aspects of the issues explored in this book, you will critically evaluate the information presented.

It is important that you decide whether you are being presented with facts or opinions. Does the writer give a biased or unbiased report? If an opinion is being expressed, do you agree with the writer? Is there potential bias to the 'facts' or statistics behind an article?

ASSIGNMENTS

In the back of this book, you will find a selection of assignments designed to help you engage with the articles you have been reading and to explore your own opinions. Some tasks will take longer than others and there is a mixture of design, writing and research-based activities that you can complete alone or in a group.

FURTHER RESEARCH

At the end of each article we have listed its source and a website that you can visit if you would like to conduct your own research. Please remember to critically evaluate any sources that you consult and consider whether the information you are viewing is accurate and unbiased.

Useful Websites

www.bankofengland.co.uk

www.blueskyifas.co.uk

www.changechecker.org

www.ecnmy.org

www.fca.org.uk

www.independent.co.uk

www.inews.co.uk

www.ipsos.com

www.moneyfacts.co.uk

www.mybnk.org

www.positivemoney.org

www.roostermoney.com

www.splitthebills.co.uk

www.telegraph.co.uk

www.thebalance.com

www.theconversation.com

www.treasurers.org

www.unherd.com

www.wearencs.com

www.unherd.com

www.yougov.co.uk

What is money?

Have you ever seen a coin that is made of totally blank, unmarked metal? All coins start like this, but at some point most get stamped or marked by a king, an emperor or a nation. Once stamped, these metal disks are suddenly transformed into money.

What's going on here? The value of metal coins has little to do with the value of the metal in the coin itself – notoriously, it costs around two pennies to make a penny in the United States. But by stamping a number on it, the government can decide exactly how much it is worth. This system, where money is valuable just because the government says it is, is called fiat money. Today our money isn't something inherently useful – like gold, salt or cigarettes. While these types of currencies consisting of items that are useful in themselves, called commodity money, have been used in the past, today almost all our money is something that would otherwise be useless.

We give money value by agreeing to use it and treat it as valuable. Otherwise, it'd just be metal, paper, and numbers on a page. As long as everyone plays along, money is accepted to be valuable, and can be used regularly to buy and sell things. That's why a 100 dollar bill can be said to be worth 100 dollars; because we all believe the fine print that says it is. This means the value of fiat money comes primarily from the trust we have in the institutions issuing and upholding it. When that trust breaks down, the consequences can be dramatic, as money quickly loses its value – this (pretty scary) process is called hyperinflation.

But coins and paper bills are only one form of money, called currency. When you think about how much money you have, you probably also count the savings you have deposited in the bank. If you have them, you might even count financial assets you own like stocks or bonds.

How do we draw lines around what counts as money and what doesn't? As you can imagine, this is a tricky question, and economists have come up with multiple definitions of money that include different things. This becomes pretty important when trying to understand how money is created because physical currency makes up a surprisingly small amount of the total money supply.

What does money do?

Money buys stuff – easy, right? Beyond this, economists have come up with some handy ways to think about what it is we do with money that help explain why it's so important to our day to day lives.

First, money is a medium of exchange which lets us earn, buy, and sell completely different things in the same units. Instead of trying to trade what we have for what we want, we are able to sell what we have for money, and then buy what we want with money. This makes money unique, and fairly central to how we get the things we need.

On top of this, money is also a unit of account – i.e. it lets us put the prices of very different things in the same terms. This lets us quantify the value of the hours we work in the same terms that we use to put value on a loaf of bread or the price of rent. People debate how far we can (or should) go in trying to express the value of things using money, particularly when it comes to placing prices on nature or living things.

Money is also used as a store of value. While other products might wear out, break, or become out of date, money generally feels like a safe way to store our savings. If you work overtime or do an extra job, you can store up your earnings, and use them later to pay for a holiday, a wedding, or the deposit on a house. Sure, you could theoretically store your savings in some other way – perhaps by collecting rare Pokémon cards – but money is probably a more safe bet. This is why it's such a big deal when the value of money unexpectedly decreases because of inflation.

Which of the above understandings of money is most important or accurate is something economists don't agree on. What we know for sure is that money is a pretty unique thing – and having a lot of it gives you quite a bit of power, not to mention freedom.

2020

When did we start using money?

There are two big ideas of how we started using money. One: money started as a solution to problems with barter between people who had to trade. Two: money was created by governments to settle debts. Who's right, and who cares?

Take the barter idea first. A long time ago, the story goes, people would swap goods for other goods (chickens for pigs, or blankets for pots) at a generally agreed upon rate (say ten chickens for a pig, or two blankets for a large pot). But because people couldn't always find someone else to swap exactly what they needed, people would come up with a convenient thing that was rare, durable and easy to standardize—like beads, shells or metal coins—and prices for pigs, chickens, blankets and pots would be translated into a given number of this special thing.

Economists like the barter story, but some anthropologists see it differently. They say the earliest historical evidence of something similar to what we call money emerged around 5000 years ago in Mesopotamia (modern-day Iraq). The bureaucrats running the royal palace needed a unit of account to measure wages, calculate taxes or fines, and settle debts between traders and landowners. Money took the form of standardized weights of silver, whose value was determined not by the value of the metal itself, but by a government decree—not unlike the banknotes we use today.

These two versions of the story of money's origins matter, because they imply different understandings of what money is and how the economy should be managed. Can people manage things like trade on their own, or do we need the government to do really basic things like making money? In the barter version of events, money emerged spontaneously from transactions between individuals, without a need for government intervention. In the Mesopotamian example, money was developed by a public institution to help people settle their debts to each other.

2021

What do banks do?

What sets high street banks apart from other businesses is the way they work with money.

High-street banks are not that different from any other business. What sets them apart is that they work with money: looking after it, lending it, and helping you pay for things with it.

Banks look after your money

Keeping small amounts of money in your pocket to pay for things makes sense. But holding larger amounts is risky as there is a chance your money could get lost or stolen.

> *Banks make sure your money is kept safe – and have served this role since ancient Greek and Roman times.*

Many banks today offer free safekeeping services, with no charge for using your current account. In return, they are able to use the money stored with them to earn a profit, by lending it to other people.

We make sure banks operate in a safe and sound way so that your money is there when you need it. And should the worst happen and your bank fails, you could claim up to £85,000 of your money back through the Financial Services Compensation Scheme

Banks lend money

Banks don't just look after your money. They also lend money to those who need it.

Banks provide loans for many things, whether you're a family looking to buy a house or a business seeking to expand, hire and grow. In this way, the flow of lending can help the economy as a whole to thrive.

Lending money is a risky business, though. Banks can lose out if someone they have lent money to doesn't pay it back.

Banks know this, so they try to make sure they earn enough profit by charging more interest for lending money than they pay out in interest on people's savings.

Of course, some loans are riskier than others – and banks will charge higher interest rates to reflect this.

But no-one can predict the future perfectly. Inevitably, banks sometimes get it wrong: sometimes a large number of loans will not be repaid. So the Bank of England makes sure that banks hold sufficient financial resources in case they face larger losses than they expect. That is part of ensuring banks operate in a safe and sound way.

Banks help you pay for things

Banks provide debit and credit cards so you can pay for things in the shops and online.

> *Over 9 in 10 adults make payments using a debit card at least once a month.*
>
> Source: UK Payments Markets 2016

When you use a card to buy, say, food, the money is transferred from your bank account to the bank account of the shop. Exactly the same thing happens when you pay for things using your debit or credit card online.

When you add to this the payments for much bigger items, like houses, and all the financial activity between banks and other financial situations, over £500 billion moves between bank accounts every single day. That's over £5 million every second.

The stakes are very high: if these payments stopped working, then the entire economy would grind to a halt. This is why the Bank of England oversees these payments - to make sure they operate smoothly every day.

What else do banks do?

Looking after your money, lending money and helping you pay for things are the main ways that people use banks in their daily lives.

Banks do other things too. Most investment banks, for example, trade shares, foreign currencies and commodities (like oil or gold) in financial markets on behalf of their clients.

> *The original meaning of "bank" comes from the Old High German word meaning "bench". Early bankers in Europe used benches as makeshift counters for banking transactions.*

2021

The history of the UK banknote

The UK banknotes have gone through some big changes since they were first introduced but do you know the story behind them? In this blog, we guide you through the history of UK banknotes as we take a look at just how far they've come…

By Alexandra Siddons from Change Checker

Timeline

7th Century – China

The first recorded use of 'paper' money was in China back in the seventh century! However, it was not until over a thousand years later that paper money made its way to Europe.

16th Century – Goldsmith-Bankers

In the 16 century, the goldsmith-bankers would issue receipts for cash, known as 'running cash notes'. They were made out in the name of the depositor and also carried the words, 'or bearer', after the name of the depositor.

This similar phrase still appears on British banknotes today: "I promise to pay the bearer on demand the sum of…"

1694 – Bank of England

When the Bank of England was established in 1694 to raise money for King William III's war effort, they issued notes in exchange for deposits. These were the first recorded bank notes to feature a cashier's signature!

18 Century – fixed denominations

The issuing of fixed denomination notes first started in the 18th century. Notes were printed with the pound sign and the first digit included, but any following digits were then added by hand!

By 1745, notes were issued in denominations ranging from £20 to £1,000 but it wasn't until 1759, as a result of gold shortages caused by the seven years of war, that a £10 note was issued.

The £5 note followed in 1793 at the start of the war against Revolutionary France and by 1797 the £1 and £2 notes were issued.

1853 – fully printed

In 1853, the first fully printed banknotes were introduced, meaning hand-written denominations on notes were phased out.

Early 20th Century – 10 shilling note

During the First World War, the link between notes and gold was broken. The government needed to preserve bullion stocks and so the Bank stopped paying out gold for its notes.

In 1914 the Treasury printed and issued 10 shilling and £1 notes and in 1931, Britain left the gold standard.

Late 20 Century – feature of historical figures

The late 20 century saw the first introduction of historical figures on the designs of UK banknotes. Since 1970, we've seen figures including scientist Isaac Newton, composer Edward Elgar and nurse Florence Nightingale featured on our banknotes.

21 Century – Polymer notes and BAME figures

In the 21 century we have seen the introduction of the polymer £5, £10 and £20 banknote, as a cleaner, safer and stronger alternative to the paper notes. These notes have become incredibly popular with collectors, with some polymer £20 notes fetching far over their face value on the secondary market!

However, a lack of Black, Asian and Minority Ethnic (BAME) figures being recognised on legal tender led to campaigning for greater inclusivity in 2020. These campaigns come after Chancellor Rishi Sunak stated he was considering proposals from a campaign group. He has since asked the Royal Mint to come up with new designs honouring BAME figures who have served the nation – such as military figures and nurses.

22 September 2020

Why financial education is so important for young people

Where should children learn their financial skills and money management?

I f a recent survey is to be believed, most parents think that it's the responsibility of schools to teach basic financial skills, and an overwhelming majority think that these subjects should be added to the curriculum.

94% of UK parents in the Portafina study want their children to be taught more financial skills at school, while almost three-quarters of parents quizzed believe their children would benefit from learning about issues such as pensions and saving at secondary school.

9 in 10 parents believe it is a school's role to provide financial education

Although most parents want their children to learn financial skills, nine in ten of them don't believe it is their responsibility to teach financial management, and that it is a school's role to provide this advice.

The study also revealed that more than two-thirds of people say that learning about money at school would have helped them in later life. The top five financial skills that British parents wish they had learned at school are:

- ◆ What a pension is and what the future benefits are (32%)
- ◆ Basic budgeting and financial management (28%)
- ◆ Ways of saving (savings accounts, ISAs etc.) (28%)
- ◆ General investment knowledge (27%)
- ◆ How interest rates work (23%)

The Personal Finance Society Education Champions scheme

To help improve financial literacy among young people, the Personal Finance Society (PFS) has launched a nationwide initiative to teach basic skills in secondary schools.

The 'Education Champions' scheme aims to provide complementary financial education for teenagers and young people, and it is hoped that it will ultimately become a key part of the national curriculum.

The initiative aims to establish an active link with every secondary school and college of further education in the country. More than 250 financial advisers and planners registered an interest in becoming a volunteer trainer within the first two days of the scheme being announced.

The PFS has created four financial education workshops in collaboration with the financial education provider 'Young Money'. These initial lessons will cover:

1. My future finances – the value of everyday expenses, setting long-term goals and evaluating these goals according to a range of incomes

2. Staying safe from scams – how to recognise different types of scams and taking steps to avoid becoming a scam victim

3. Moving on from school – explaining a payslip, how income deductions work, how to calculate gross and net income, and how the government uses taxes and National Insurance Contributions

4. Making decisions and risk – understanding financial risks, why people take risks with money, the difference between 'low' and 'high' risk, and how insurance and other methods can be used to protect against financial risks.

While these sessions are set to help young people improve their financial skills, there are also steps you can take as a parent or grandparent to help a child to learn more about money. Here are a few suggestions.

5 important things you can teach your children or grandchildren about money

1. Spending vs saving

One of the simplest lessons you can teach children is about 'spending versus saving'. Do they spend their cash immediately, or save up to buy something more valuable?

Gary Edwards, founder of primary school financial education firm Keep On Squirrelling, says: "Our mantra is keep half, spend half. This is something children can apply now, as they do not have the large outgoings adults may have. If they carry this principle into adulthood, it will transform their life financially."

2. Compound interest

Albert Einstein once famously said: "Compound interest is the eighth wonder of the world. He who understands it, earns it… he who doesn't, pays it."

The idea of earning interest on interest can be hard to understand, but, when explained, it can help children to think about saving long-term. This is particularly important when they start to think about putting money aside for their retirement.

3. Money is earned

One of the most important lessons to teach a child is about the value of money. One way of doing this is to ensure that children earn any money that they receive, meaning they make the link between working and earning.

Becky O'Connor, Personal Finance Specialist at Royal London, says: "Don't give pocket money without requiring your child to do something for it."

4. Long-term saving and pensions

In a similar vein to teaching a child about compound interest, you can show them the difference between long-term savings and cash investments. For example, show them how much better a pension fund has performed than a savings account.

Don't forget that you can even set up a pension for your child or grandchild. You can pay up to £2,880 each year into the pension of an under 18-year-old, and with the £720 tax relief the pension provider claims from the government, the pension fund could grow by £3,600 every year.

Bear in mind that the child won't be able to access the pension until they come to retire later, meaning they can't cash in the fund to put down a deposit on a home, for example.

5. Manage expectations

A Halifax survey of 1,000 schoolchildren found that many of them overestimate the salaries of certain professions. For example, they thought that teachers earn £140,000 a year and police officers £165,000 a year, when the reality is that starting salaries for these jobs is around £23,000.

Becky O'Connor from Royal London suggests that you should give children examples of people they admire and earn a lot to help them understand the concept of commitment and hard work. "After all, Lionel Messi didn't earn his money watching TV all day," she says.

17 September 2019

Why spending money can make you happy

A string of studies show that spending your income can really boost your mental wellbeing.

By Marina Gerner

Those who say money can't buy happiness may not be spending it the right way. A budding field of behavioural science is analysing how our spending decisions influence our wellbeing.

We explain how money can buy happiness – if you follow the right principles.

One morning, people on the streets of Vancouver were asked to take part in an experiment by Harvard Business School researchers led by professors Elizabeth Dunn and Michael Norton. Those who agreed to take part received an envelope containing either $5 (£4) or $20 (£15).

They were asked how happy they were and instructed to spend the money by 5pm. Crucially, half of the group was told to spend it on themselves, while the other half were told to donate to charity or buy a present or spend it on somebody else.

Measurably happier

That evening, each respondent received a phone call from the researchers. They were was asked how happy they felt and how they had spent their money.

People from the first group had bought themselves coffee from Starbucks, sushi and even earrings.

The second group had bought toys for younger relatives, given money to homeless people or bought coffee for someone else.

How did these purchases make them feel? It turned out that the amount of money people discovered in the envelopes didn't matter. Exactly what they bought didn't matter either. What did matter, was who they spent it on.

Those who were asked to spend money on others were measurably happier at the end of the day than those who spent it on themselves.

Buy experiences rather than things

Millennials are often said to prefer spending money on experiences over material goods. And research suggests they are on to something.

Studies show that spending money on experiences makes us happier than spending it on material goods.

"You buy furniture to convey an image of who you are," says Thomas Gilovich, a professor of psychology at Cornell University in New York. Material things don't define us the way experiences do.

Think of an unforgettable play at the theatre or a trip to see the northern lights.

"Experiences loom large in the narrative of our life," notes Prof Gilovich.

Telling a compelling story about ourselves is core to wellbeing. What's more, developing skills through experiences gives us pleasure as mastering our environment makes sense from an evolutionary perspective.

Use money to 'buy time'

We say that time is money, but is it actually the other way around? Despite rising incomes, people increasingly feel pressed for time, which undermines their wellbeing, according to Ashley Whillans, a professor at Harvard Business School.

Once people make more than enough to meet their basic needs, additional money does not bring greater happiness. Yet our choices do not reflect this. Prof Whillans found that the majority of people – including millionaires – tend to prioritise having more money over more time.

Prof Whillans then surveyed more than 6,000 working adults in the Netherlands, Denmark, US and Canada and found that people "who spent money on time-saving services reported greater satisfaction with their lives".

This includes paying someone else to do disliked household chores such as cleaning and cooking.

It also means we should think twice before accepting a better paid job with a longer commute, or a marginally cheaper flight that would require more waiting around.

The personality test

Researchers at the University of Cambridge asked 625 participants to fill out a personality test. Then, they asked them to ascribe traits to things they might spend money on – like books, coffee, insurance, pets and clothes – as if they were people.

Pubs, they decided, are outgoing and a bit impulsive. Home insurance is reserved and dependable. And gift shops are even-tempered.

The researchers then culled 76,000 bank transactions of these participants for six months. They analysed how similar each participant's personality was to that of their shopping basket's character. The result: "personality-matched consumption" results in higher levels of happiness.

In other words, extroverts are happier to receive a voucher for a bar, while introverts prefer a gift card or a bookshop.

So the secret to happiness? Make sure that you spend money on others, prioritise experiences over things, use money to buy time – and spend it in a way that suits your personality and values.

28 February 2020

Love and money: how to avoid differing attitudes towards finance causing disasters in your love life

For women in particular, it's a tricky subject to navigate, but it doesn't have to be a deal-breaker.

By Alys Key

I was working on a story recently about people who follow the FIRE lifestyle – an extreme method of saving and investing aimed at making early retirement possible – when one of my interviewees mentioned her love life.

"This whole movement kind of limits your dating" said Laura Poole, 27. "If I meet someone and find out they tend to go into debt over Christmas, that's a deal-breaker."

While not everyone is committed to such an intense money regime, the idea of mismatched attitudes to money scuppering relationships is an interesting one.

I turned to Hayley Quinn, dating expert at match.com, for help looking closer at this topic. "Tensions can arise over money right from the first day, or might only become apparent when things get serious," she says.

First dates are littered with potential moments which expose different approaches to money, from talking about holidays to discussing jobs. And then of course, there's the age-old question: shall we go Dutch?

The early warning signs

Hayley says that many people still cite splitting the bill as a dating bugbear. If the daters are a man and a woman, is it sexist to expect the man to pay? Is asking to pay just for your own share an indication that the date isn't going well? Should you limit your order to make sure the bill doesn't get too high?

"In my opinion, there isn't a right or a wrong answer," says Hayley. "But having an incompatible attitude towards the answer could mean you're not well suited."

She suggests that different approaches say something about the person's philosophy. "Some people will prefer to pick up the tab because it shows generosity; and while some of their dates may prefer (or expect) to be treated, others will find not splitting the bill old fashioned."

Rebecca, 26, from London, was quick to realise that her now-girlfriend was in a different financial situation than her own. "I clocked my girlfriend had money when she mentioned – in the first 20 minutes of our first date – that she was considering buying a house. It wasn't awkward, but it was interesting – she is now horrified she said that."

Hayley says there is a stereotype that young people do not think as much about finances in their dating life because "they prioritise experiences over equity". While it can be true, she says it is not the same for everyone. Especially now that the UK is officially in recession again, young people are hyper-aware of economic inequality.

Although money is an issue across different age groups, being in different life stages can certainly lead to unaligned expectations for who spends what in a relationship.

Amy, who is in her late 20s, has a partner in his late 30s who already has children. "I was a bit naïve," she says. "I simply didn't realise how much children cost, and I probably let him pay for more than he could really afford.

"Money was never an issue until we started thinking about a long-term relationship. Half his income goes straight to the children, which is as it should be, but it does make financial planning more complicated."

This is consistent with the experiences of other couples, according to Hayley. "Money issues can tend to crop up after the initial honeymoon period has ended and you encounter bigger life planning questions around mortgages, career choices and children," she says. "If one person is a saver and the other prefers to live in the moment this conflict could end up spilling out into other areas of the relationship."

Feeling the strain

Amy has had this exact same issue. "He definitely isn't as careful or as aware of money as I am. That kind of pressure is more stressful than I anticipated it would be," she says. "But overall, even if I had known about how complicated merging finances would be at the start, I wouldn't have done anything differently."

If both Amy and Rebecca were able to overcome differences of income and form happy relationships, does that mean money doesn't matter?

"You are highly unlikely to meet someone who shares exactly the same attitude as you in everything, and even if you do, it could be quite boring," says Hayley. "What's more important than being 100 per cent in agreement all the time, is having tolerance and understanding of one another when you don't agree."

The subject can be particularly fraught for women who date men. Holding on to your independence while building a life with someone is difficult for anyone, but given the history of women relying on male partners for money, it can make some women feel uncomfortable.

For Lynn, who is in her mid-50s, it was more important to prioritise her self-sufficiency: "I lived with someone who, on paper, is a woman's dream. Six-bedroom house, paid for everything. I could have whatever I wanted but I've run my own home since I was 18 and after living like this for two years I'm moving out."

At first it looked like the relationship would end, but her partner has since accepted her decision to live separately. "Moving out has done wonders for our sex life," she says. "And he now knows that if I say I'm going to do something, I do it."

4 September 2020

UK pocket money index 2021

The Pocket Money Index is a snapshot of the pocket money habits of kids aged 4-14 across the UK. Whether it's the average allowance given per week, or what the top earning chores are, you can find it all here.

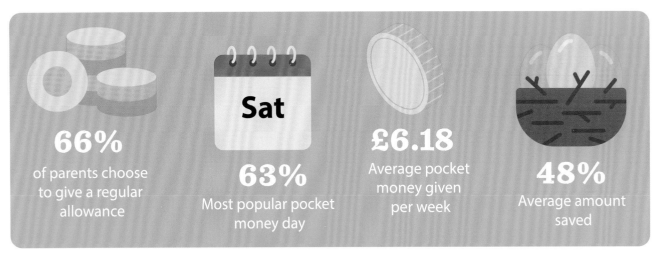

66%
of parents choose to give a regular allowance

Sat
63%
Most popular pocket money day

£6.18
Average pocket money given per week

48%
Average amount saved

Average pocket money by age

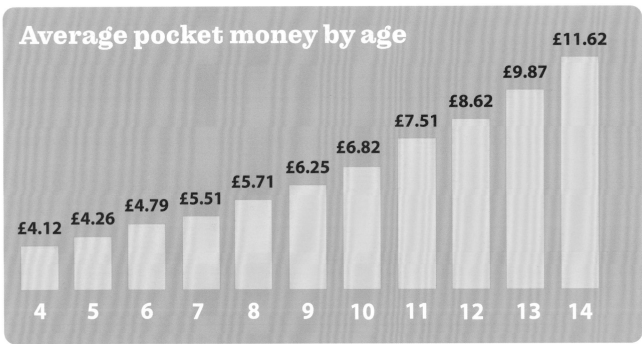

Age	Amount
4	£4.12
5	£4.26
6	£4.79
7	£5.51
8	£5.71
9	£6.25
10	£6.82
11	£7.51
12	£8.62
13	£9.87
14	£11.62

Where's it coming from?

Most common chores
1. Tidying the bedroom
2. Emptying the dishwasher
3. Making the bed
4. Doing the laundry
5. Hoovering

Top paid chores
1. Washing the car   £2.97
2. Mowing the lawn   £2.67
3. Washing windows   £1.78
4. Raking leaves   £1.78
5. Cleaning bathroom   £1.24

Extra earners
Tooth Fairy visit

Found somewhere

Being good

School report

Getting good grades: £2.23

Doing homework £0.65

Highest earning subject: **MATHS**

Generous family members

Average given
£22.30

The big earner

Birthdays

£43.17

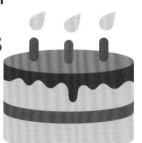

Pet care

Feeding cats

£0.37

Feeding dogs

£0.34

Where's it going?

Top 5 things to spend on

1. Roblox

2. Lego

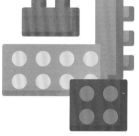

3. Books & mags

4. Fortnite

5. PlayStation

Top 5 things to save for

1. Phone

2. Lego

3. Nintendo

4. PlayStation

5. Roblox

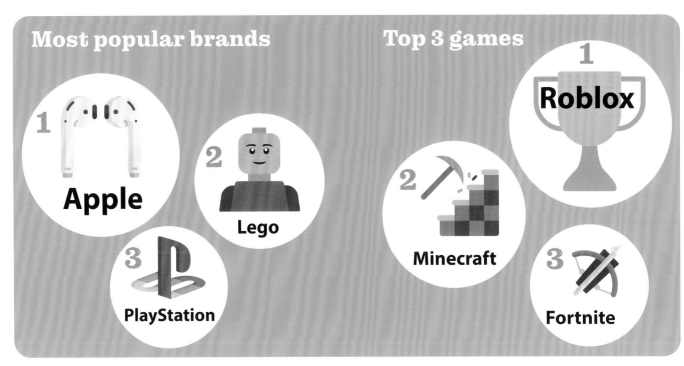

Most popular brands

1 **Apple**

2 Lego

3 PlayStation

Top 3 games

1 **Roblox**

2 Minecraft

3 Fortnite

Top 3 charitable causes chosen by kids

1 **Comic Relief**

2 **National Trust**

3 **WWF**

Top stores

1. Amazon

2. Co-op

3. Xbox

4. Sainsbury's

5. Google Play Store

6. PlayStation

7. Apple App Store

8. Xsolta

9. Poundland

10. Shein.com

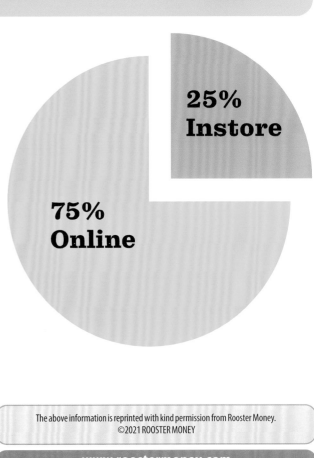

25% Instore

75% Online

Children as young as four are spending money online

The survey of 2,000 parents found 12 per cent had experienced their pre-school children spending money online despite their young ages.

By Charles Hymas, Home Affairs Editor

Children as young as four are spending money online despite tech firms' claims that they are "safe" for children so young, a study has found.

The survey of 2,000 parents found 12 per cent had experienced their pre-school children spending money online despite their young ages.

Internet Matters, a body that supports parents, said they were often free games advertised as suitable for children of that age, but which then went on to request payments from the youngsters to advance to another level, or buy equipment that could boost their character's performance.

Ghislaine Bombusa, head of digital at Internet Matters, said children often played them on shared or parental devices which meant the child could access payments or agree it with their parents.

"We advise parents that if they are downloading something onto a shared device or onto their own device, they should have a good look around it and check it," said Ms Bombusa.

"If you are not able to get the information that you need or it appears to be hiding the fact that it requires spending but claims to be free, then that's a problem. That's where we advise that if there is insufficient information, don't download it."

The survey also revealed that nearly one in 12 (eight per cent) of four and five year olds had stumbled across sexual content.

A similar proportion (seven per cent) had suffered online trolling or abuse by strangers, while one in eight (13 per cent) had viewed violent content.

The survey found more than two in five parents (43 per cent) were concerned about their children spending money online in games and apps.

There was also concern among parents that children were being tempted into gambling with loot boxes that offered the chance of digital add-ons for their characters in return for cash.

Almost two in five (38 per cent) parents were concerned with their children gambling on websites or in games and/or apps.

Dr Linda Papadopoulos, child psychologist and Internet Matters ambassador, said: "While children may know their way round the latest online video game, many are in over their heads when it comes to understanding the value of money, which is why we see so many headlines about kids accidentally racking up thousands of pounds online.

"Just like it's natural for us to advise children how to spend their pocket money in the offline world, we need to help them in the online world. It's important for us to have conversations with them about the risks of spending money online and how they might be susceptible to fraud, scams or other financial harms.

"Also talk to your child about peer pressure they might feel. We know from recent reports that kids have spent hundreds of pounds on items such as loot boxes where they are unsure of the rewards just to keep up with their friends."

Internet Matters has launched a new hub to help parents address the issue of children's online money management.

The new guides, released on Tuesday, include advice on in-game spending and new trends such as gifting gaming influencers and buying loot boxes.

14 April 2021

Teenagers are now spending half of their pocket money on gambling, report finds

By Lizzie Roberts

Teenagers are now spending half of their pocket money on gambling, according to data released by the Gambling Commission.

Eleven to 16-year-olds who admitted to gambling said they spent £17 per week on games, such as fruit machines and online "loot boxes", equalling half of their weekly allowance of £34.

The figures show young people are now gambling over 50 percent more compared to two years ago, when the same group said they spent just £10 per week on the vice.

The most common types of gambling young people engage in are making private bets or playing cards for money, playing fruit or slot machines and buying National Lottery scratch cards, the survey found.

Around 3,000 11 to 16-year-olds took part in the study, via online surveys completed in school, and around one in ten said they spent their own money on gambling in the past seven days.

More than half of the children surveyed had heard of in-game items, such as weapons, power-ups and tokens, and 44 percent had said they had paid money to open loot boxes.

This week Anne Longfield, the Children's Commissioner, warned "loot boxes", in which gamers are offered the chance to buy random in-game items online, should be classified as a form of gambling and banned for children.

Ms Longfield said: "Children are open to exploitation by games companies who play on their need to keep up with friends and to advance to further stages of a game by encouraging children to spend on loot boxes."

The Gambling Commission has previously warned the gambling of "skins" - in-game digital items used to alter a gamer's appearance - among children is a "new phenomenon" of "considerable concern".

They urge parents and guardians to be vigilant of the practice, and report any unlicensed "skins gambling" sites via their confidential hotline.

More than two-thirds of the young people surveyed, 69 percent, said they had seen or heard gambling ads or sponsorship, but 83 percent of these said it had not prompted them to gamble.

Gambling Commission executive director, Tim Miller, said: "Most of the gambling covered by this report takes place in ways which the law permits but we must keep working to prevent children and young people from having access to age restricted products.

"Where operators have failed to protect children and young people, we have and will continue to take firm action.

"Protecting children and young people from gambling harms is a collective responsibility and requires us, other regulators, the government, gambling operators, charities, teachers and parents to work together to make progress."

Over the past 12 months the number of young people who said they spent money on gambling fell to 36 percent, from 39 percent in 2018.

The Gambling Commission said the percentage of young people classified as "problem" gamblers was unchanged from last year at 1.7 percent, although the percentage classified as "at risk" has risen from 2.2 percent to 2.7 percent.

Last year the Commission called on the pub industry to take action after 21 percent of young people said they had played fruit machines in a pub.

This year the same figure had dropped to 11 percent.

23 October 2019

Magic Money Tree

Politicians often like to point out that there is no "magic money tree". But that raises the question, where does money actually come from? The answer is more complicated than many people realise.

If you listened to some government ministers, you might assume that there's a fixed amount of money in the economy, or that the amount is strictly controlled by the Bank of England.

But in fact, money is being created out of thin air all the time. And this process has hugely important implications for issues like housing, inequality and the environment.

Most of the money we use comes in digital form, as the numbers we see on our bank statements. This money is created by private banks like HSBC and Natwest when they make loans. They create it by simply typing numbers into a computer – some might call this magic!

Sound implausible? You don't have to take our word for it – the Bank of England itself has confirmed that "whenever a bank makes a loan, it creates a deposit in the borrower's bank account, thereby creating new money."

Unfortunately, banks direct most of their lending towards property and financial speculation, which pushes up house prices and makes financial crises more likely. Banks prefer lending to the 'financial' economy than the 'real' economy, where most ordinary people would see the benefit. This means they do a bad job of lending to businesses which create jobs and grow the economy in a sustainable way.

And because commercial banks were slow to start lending again after the 2008 crisis, the Bank of England stepped in with its own money creation programme called quantitative easing. It's chosen to pump this new money into the financial sector, which is pushing up the value of assets like houses, shares, and corporate bonds.

This policy has done very little for ordinary people, but the Bank of England's own research has shown that quantitative easing made the richest 5% over £128,000 richer. So at a time when politicians are using the absence of a "magic money tree" to justify austerity, the Bank of England policies are enriching a wealthy few.

All of this exposes how dysfunctional our money and banking system is. But we know it doesn't have to be this way. We can reform the system so that it supports a fairer and more sustainable economy.

Instead of the Bank of England pumping new money into financial markets through quantitative easing, it should be spent via the government into infrastructure, green technology, or as a cash transfer to help households pay off their debts and improve their finances.

And we need to transform our banking system so that banks lend money to support investment and jobs in the real economy. This means having a more diverse range of banks and government policies that encourage lending for productive purposes.

2020

Spending vs. saving: how to find the perfect balance

Becoming financially independent for the first time can be an exciting but overwhelming time. Whether you've received your first pay cheque or student loan instalment, it can be tempting to spend it all at once. But in reality, you'll need to dedicate a significant portion of your income to rent, food and bills.

Research shows that 78% of students worry about making ends meet. Despite this, one in five have never budgeted.

After the essential costs have been paid, it's important to devise a plan of how to utilise any spare money. Instead of impulse spending, you'll thank yourself later for learning how to balance saving for your future with buying the occasional treat.

Bring in the experts

To find out the best ways to budget, save and spend money we decided to seek advice from the experts.

Caroline Domanska—income strategist and founder of Money Mindset Coach

Dennis Harhalakis—founder of Cambridge Money Coaching

Ashley Tate—chief executive officer at online student bill-sharing tool Split The Bills

Claire Roach—money-saving blogger and owner of Daily Deals UK

Learn how to budget

Being aware of your fundamental expenses is the first way to take control of your finances. This will help you avoid spending beyond your means and reach long-term goals.

Recent findings from NatWest revealed that 42% of students don't use any budgeting methods to help their money go further and 6% said they don't consider what they're spending at all.

Claire: "Every single student I know has blown most of their student loan on holidays, nights out and new clothes. The best way to avoid this is to plan your budget in advance."

To begin your financial plan, assess your monthly income. This is especially vital if you work freelance or rely on tips. If you earn more than expected or have a slow month, it could affect your budget for the following month.

Use a notebook, online spreadsheet or budgeting app to make a note of your monthly financial obligations and subtract this amount from your income.

Claire: "Ensure you pay your bills and make any essential purchases the day you get paid so you don't have lots of cash in your bank account to tempt you into non-essential spending."

This can include rent, bills, student loan payments and insurance premiums.

Ashley: "Seeing your spending habits written down can be a wake-up call. If your budget amount outweighs your income, something needs to go. Be honest with yourself about what you can actually afford and what you can live without.

"The budget might highlight areas you could cut costs. Small purchases, like a takeaway lunch or a morning coffee, might seem harmless but they can add up to a surprisingly large fee."

After factoring these vital payments into your budget, your next priority might be fixed-cost automated payments such as a Netflix subscription or gym membership.

Dennis said: "Most of it is common sense and maths, but budgeting is also an emotional process which can be challenging. It's also difficult if you're flat-sharing with friends or a partner who might have different views and priorities."

When you begin the next month's budget, consider what worked and what didn't. You might decide to make adjustments as time goes on if your financial priorities change.

Organise utility costs

Be aware of how much your utility bills cost, and keep track of any changes. This can be tricky if someone else is responsible for organising these payments. But being oblivious to the exact amount could result in overspending and not having enough to cover the cost.

It may also be beneficial to create a joint account so that everyone can easily check outgoings. But only do this with people who are financially secure and can be trusted to pay on time.

Ashley: "If you share a joint account with someone who has bad credit, makes late payments or if the account goes overdrawn it could impact your credit score. This could stop you from getting a mortgage or even a mobile phone contract in the future."

If all payments come out of one person's bank account, it can be difficult for everyone to keep track of the costs. If anybody doesn't transfer their share of the bills on time, the responsibility falls onto the account holder.

Ashley: "If you find it difficult to keep on top of numerous different bills, use a billsplitting service that puts all utilities into one monthly payment for each person. Only having one cost to consider makes budgeting much simpler."

How much should you save?

If you have any money left over, envisage your saving goals and work them into your budget.

Caroline: "I'd look at all the things that are important to you in the short, medium and long term and allocate some money to each. Put some money in a different bank account that's harder for you to access."

Saving while you're young will make things much easier when you're ready to buy a house, get married or are in desperate need of a holiday.

Caroline: "I think Millennials do save but, in my experience, they don't know what to do with the money and the housing market, so the money just sits in cash and then tempts spending."

A report from last year found that 53% of 22- to 29-year-olds had no money set aside in a savings account or an ISA (individual savings account) between 2014 and 2016.

Caroline: "My philosophy is that you can spend your money how you like, but ideally you could be doing a little bit of everything. It's this idea of balance and starting small that should be promoted.

"Even if it feels impossible to save for a house or pointless saving for retirement, if you start with something—even £25—it opens the door to the possibility of it happening, and allows you to work on a plan to increase these contributions over time."

Allow yourself occasional treats

Saving is important, but if it forces you to abandon your social life, hobbies or love for new things, you'll most likely feel deprived. This can result in reckless, unplanned and impulsive spending.

Dennis: "A good guide is to allocate 50% to needs, 30% to wants and 20% to saving. Automate the savings process and only spend what's left over. If you want to control your spending, set a weekly allowance, take it out in cash and leave the cards at home."

Saving less so that you can afford the occasional treat could actually lead to more money being saved in the long run.

Caroline: "Have a fun pot. I'd suggest putting 5-10% of your income into here every month and don't be afraid to use it. But remember once it's gone, it's gone."

Eliminate bad spending habits

Treating yourself to the occasional swanky dinner or new outfit may seem harmless, but try not to get carried away and always stick to the allocated amount in your budget.

Ashley: "Due to the peer pressure young people often face, or urge to compare ourselves when scrolling social media, it's hard not to turn to material goods to feel better and develop irresponsible spending behaviour."

Online platforms such as Instagram and YouTube are brimming with sponsored and aspirational content which constantly encourages people to spend.

Claire: "Social media is so powerful these days. For millennials, it's a massive part of their everyday lives. From perfect holidays to perfect outfits, there's always someone posting their new purchases, which the impressionable younger generation try to live up to."

Australian research from last year discovered 88% of students say social media has some impact on their spending habits, and over a third of students cited FOMO (fear of missing out) and peer pressure from social media as spending triggers.

Caroline: "We often have a false impression of how others live their life. We can assume they have the money to pay for what we see, but it's not always the case."

In the 2018 Student Lifestyle Survey, 74% of students said they bought new clothes and shoes before moving to university.

Caroline: "Education is needed about living life in your own lane and learning what makes you—not someone else—feel first class. Choose to spend your money in a way that feels good to you."

Despite what you see on Instagram, most people can't afford to live the life of luxury. But no matter what other people are buying, it's crucial that you don't get swayed to spend irresponsibly. By creating a money management plan, you will find financial stability and prevent making messy mistakes that could land you in tremendous debt.

2020

Is too much money a bad thing?

By Peter Franklin

Some people have so much money that they struggle to find things to spend it on. But these people are paupers compared to those who run out of opportunities to invest the money they don't spend.

Yes, I know the heart bleeds – but there really is a global shortage of places for the seriously rich to put their Earthly riches. There just aren't enough alternatives to the bog standard option of the bank account.

Indeed, interest rates wouldn't be at record lows around the world if there weren't a global glut of cash.

Writing for Axios, Dion Rabouin notes that US companies have "record cash holdings of close to $3 trillion". Wealthy individuals aren't doing too badly either:

"The top 1% of U.S. households are holding a record $303.9 billion of cash, a quantum leap from the under $15 billion they held just before the financial crisis."

Of course, most of us would love to have this 'problem'. And, in a way, we do. Though the non-wealthy have little or no share in the global money glut, our lives are affected by what happens to it.

Those charged with managing extreme wealth are channeling the cash into places where it can do more harm than good – for instance, the property market where it inflates house prices and rental values. Then there's the practice of share buyback – in which cash-rich companies buy up their own stock:

"Companies made a record $1.1 trillion in stock buybacks in 2018 and are on track to surpass that number this year."

Buybacks increase demand and reduce supply, thus pushing up share prices – already inflated by the effects of quantitative easing. The executives can say they've 'added value' and are rewarded accordingly – not least in the form of 'tax efficient' stock options.

Admittedly, the company wouldn't have the cash for the buybacks if it wasn't profitable in the first place – but that's not difficult when you can borrow money at rock bottom rates (QE again), buy up the competition and exploit a monopoly position. The company's soaring market capitalisation means that the banks are happy to keep lending it money… and so on and on it goes, generating further surpluses of cash for the fortunate few.

Obviously, none of this is good for the long-term health of the economy – and, for most of us, it's of no short-term benefit either. What, then, can we do about it? Taxation is an obvious weapon, but the thing about enormous piles of cash under professional management in a borderless world is that they don't sit still waiting to be punitively taxed.

A slightly different approach is to use tax to disincentivise some of the less desirable uses of the money glut. Property-based assets are an obvious target, because it's not like we'll end up with less land if we scare away the speculators. Targeting share buybacks is trickier. While we might want

to discourage this and other forms of 'financial engineering', we also want to encourage equity investment in productive enterprise – and the finance industry is full of people who can disguise the former as the latter.

Ideally, we'd have such an enterprising, innovative economy that there'd be ample opportunities to invest in growth-generating industries. Established companies would be so threatened by new competitors that they'd invest their profits in business development instead of the complacency of share buybacks. It would also be good to have more rich people with the brains, balls and heart to invest their money imaginatively, courageously and philanthropically. That'd mop up the money glut.

Needless to say, these happy scenarios depend on culture change – which, if it happens at all, is a long-term process. So, in the meantime, is there anything that the state can do to attract excess capital into socially-useful investments?

Visionary public funding programmes of the kind that gave the internet its start are great – but, again, it's a long-term process. Fortunately, there are some quicker wins to be had – areas where strategic state-led investment can unlock avenues for productive private investment.

Consider the decades of under-investment in the economic infrastructure of our cities beyond London. Addressing key weaknesses – like the state of our non-Londoncentric public transport system – does not require futuristic technologies,

but tried-and-tested upgrades that more productive local economies already have.

The challenge for government – including local government – is to become a credible enabler of private sector investment opportunities. That means an end to the imprudence of politically-driven mega-projects like HS2 and Hinkley point, and a pivot to smaller, less complicated, productivity improvements.

The fact that so much potential has been left locked-up for so long is an indictment of our over-centralised political system and our lopsided national economy. But that can be changed – indeed, it is being changed as local communities are re-empowered and the foundations of a modern industrial policy are put in place.

A new prime minister has an opportunity to shift this work into a higher gear.

24 June 2019

UK debt reaches record high as goverment borrowing hits £19.1bn

'Coronavirus has caused one of the largest economic shocks this country has ever faced,' chancellor says.

By Samuel Osborne

The UK's debt has reached a new high as government borrowing hit £19.1bn last month as it continues to battle the coronavirus pandemic and the economic fallout of lockdown.

The Office for National Statistics (ONS) said the public sector had borrowed more last month than during any other February since records began in 1993.

The debt owed by public bodies has increased by £333bn since the start of April, the first month of full lockdown in the UK.

It brings the total debt to £2.131 trillion, the ONS said.

Central government bodies are believed to have spent around £72.6bn running their day-to-day activities in February, a rise of £14.2bn compared with February 2020. The figure includes £3.9bn spent on supporting jobs through Covid-19.

The chancellor of the exchequer, Rishi Sunak, pledged early on in the pandemic to provide whatever support businesses needed to help them through the government-imposed lockdowns.

Mr Sunak said: "Coronavirus has caused one of the largest economic shocks this country has ever faced, which is why we responded with our £352bn package of support to protect lives and livelihoods.

"This was the fiscally responsible thing to do and the best way to support the public finances in the medium-term.

"But I have always said that we should look to return the public finances to a more sustainable path once the economy has recovered and at the Budget I set out how we will begin to do just that, providing families and businesses with certainty."

The government has backed more than £70bn through three loan schemes, and also paid 80 per cent of salaries to around 10 million workers who were furloughed.

The government has relied heavily on borrowing to be able to fund this spending as tax receipts have also gone down during the period.

However, Mr Sunak has signalled that tax rises are likely in the coming years, already announcing a plan to increase corporation tax from 19 per cent to 25 per cent for large companies by 2023.

19 March 2021

Modern monetary theory: the rise of economists who say huge government debt is not a problem

An article from The Conversation.

By John Whittaker

THE CONVERSATION

There is no limit to the quantity of money that can be created by a central bank such as the Bank of England. It was different in the days of the gold standard, when central banks were restrained by a promise to redeem their money for gold on demand. But countries moved away from this system in the early part of the 20th century, and central banks nowadays can issue as much money as they like.

This observation is the root of modern monetary theory (MMT), which has attracted new attention during the pandemic, as governments around the world increase spending and public debts become all the more burdensome.

MMT proponents argue that governments can spend as necessary on all desirable causes – reducing unemployment, green energy, better healthcare and education – without worrying about paying for it with higher taxes or increased borrowing. Instead, they can pay using new money from their central bank. The only limit, according to this view, is if inflation starts to rise, in which case the solution is to increase taxes.

MMT's roots

The ideas behind MMT were mainly developed in the 1970s, notably by Warren Mosler, an American investment fund manager, who is also credited with doing much to popularise it. However, there are many threads that can be traced further back, for instance to an early 20th-century group called the chartalists, who were interested in explaining why currencies had value.

These days, prominent supporters of MMT include L Randall Wray, who teaches regular courses on the theory at Bard college in Hudson, New York state. Another academic, Stephanie Kelton, has gained the ear of politicians such as Bernie Sanders and, more recently, Democrat US presidential candidate Joe Biden, providing theoretical justification for expanding government spending.

There are more strands to MMT besides the idea that governments don't need to worry overly about spending. For instance, supporters advocate job guarantees, where the state creates jobs for unemployed people. They also argue that the purpose of taxation is not, as mainstream economics would have it, to pay for government spending, but to give people a purpose for using money: they have to use it to pay their tax.

But if we overlook these points, the main policy implication of MMT is not so controversial. It is not too far from the current new-Keynesian orthodoxy which advises that if there is unemployment, this can be cured by stimulating the economy – either through monetary policy, which focuses on cutting interest rates; or through the fiscal policies of lower taxes and higher spending.

Against this position is the monetarist doctrine that inflation is caused by too much money, and the common belief that too much government debt is bad. These two principles explain why central banks are strongly focused on inflation targets (2% in the UK), while the aversion to debt in the UK and elsewhere was the driving force behind the "austerity" policy of cutting government spending to reduce the deficit – at least until the coronavirus pandemic made governments change direction.

UK public debt as a % GDP

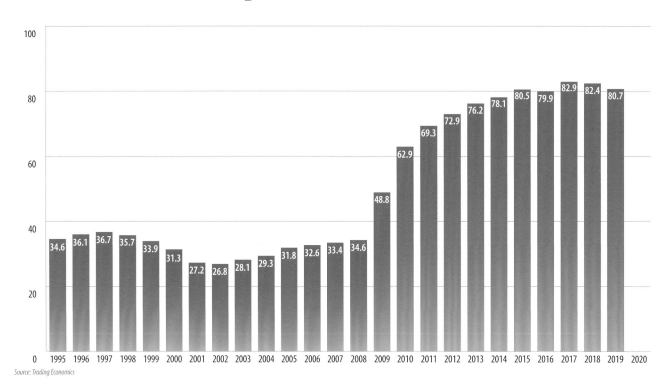

Source: Trading Economics

The crux

So, who is right – the MMT school or the fiscal and monetary conservatives? In particular, is it sensible to pay for government spending with central bank money?

When a government spends more than it receives in taxation, it has to borrow, which it usually does by selling bonds to private sector investors such as pension funds and insurance companies. Yet since 2009, the central banks of the UK, US, the eurozone, Japan and other countries have been buying large amounts of these bonds from the private-sector holders, paying for their purchases with newly created money. The purpose of this so-called "quantitative easing" (QE) has been to stimulate economic activity and to prevent deflation, and it has been greatly expanded in response to the pandemic.

At present in the UK, over £600 billion or 30% of government debt is effectively financed by central bank money – this is the value of government bonds now held by the Bank of England as a result of QE. There are similar high proportions in the other countries that have been undertaking QE.

Despite all this creation of new central bank money and the large increase in government debt in the UK and other large economies since the financial crisis of 2007-09, nowhere has there been a problem with inflation. Indeed, Japan has struggled for three decades to raise its inflation rate above zero. This evidence – that neither large debt nor large money creation has caused inflation – seems to vindicate the MMT policy recommendation to spend.

Trading Economics

Of course, there are many counterexamples in which these conditions have been associated with hyperinflation, such as Argentina in 1989, Russia at the breakup of the Soviet Union, and more recently Zimbabwe and Venezuela. But in all these cases there was an assortment of additional problems such as government corruption or instability, a history of defaults on government debt, and an inability to borrow in the country's own currency. Thankfully, the UK does not suffer from these problems.

Since the outbreak of the coronavirus pandemic, UK government spending has been rapidly increasing. Debt is now about £2 trillion or 100% of GDP. And the Bank of England, under its latest QE programme, has been buying up UK government bonds almost as fast as the government is issuing them.

Thus the crucial question is: will inflation remain subdued? Or will this vast new increase in QE-financed government spending finally cause inflation to take off, as the easing of lockdown releases pent-up demand?

If there is inflation, the Bank of England's task will be to choke it off by raising interest rates, and/or reversing QE. Or the government could try out the MMT proposal to stifle the inflation with higher taxes. The trouble is that all these responses will also depress economic activity. In such circumstances, the MMT doctrine of free spending will not look so attractive after all.

7 July 2020

Financial wellbeing – can we spot the signs of money worries?

What does it mean to be 'financially well'? Is it having a large bank balance and not getting into debt? Or is it not about how much money you have but rather how comfortable you feel? The answer is not straightforward and, to a large extent, will depend on who you ask. But research in this field has huge potential and poses new challenges for firms and regulators.

By Jeroen Nieboer and Karthik Raghavan

A feeling of financial wellbeing – feeling comfortable or free from worry – is obviously a subjective feeling. But how well does it map onto objective facts about people's financial circumstances and behaviour? Is it as simple as having more money that will bring a feeling of financial wellbeing? Or are there other factors at work and other signs that might indicate a distressed consumer?

We wanted to know whether people's everyday financial behaviour (payments, transfers in and out of their account, mobile banking logins, credit use, and so forth) could help us predict how financially well they feel.

Our research, carried out jointly with academic expert Joe Gladstone, involved asking 2,695 current account holders about how much 'money management stress' they said they were feeling in everyday life. This was then compared to their current account records over an 11 month period - with their consent and with data anonymised, naturally.

Signs of stress

The study examined what behaviours correlated with feelings of 'money management stress'. Some behaviours were essentially neutral. So, for example we found little or no correlation between people's age or gender and their reported levels of financial stress. Interestingly, income volatility also showed little correlation with financial stress. Irregular earnings do not necessarily match higher stress.

However, a number of behaviours or circumstances showed strong correlations. Some of these were as expected: people with higher incomes or higher bank balances, for example, reported fewer feelings of money management stress, while on the other hand, there was a strong correlation between the amount of time spent overdrawn and feelings of stress.

There were also some less-expected correlations. There was, for example a modest correlation between how frequently people logged on to a mobile banking app and higher levels of financial stress. And while income volatility showed little correlation with stress, account balance volatility showed a quite strong correlation. One possible explanation for this is that wellbeing is affected by mismatches in the timing of income and expenditure. Or maybe simply looking at income fluctuations in account data does not do justice to the full complexity of people's financial situations?

Either way, this is an area where innovative research with banking data could make a tangible difference, arguably now more than ever with the Covid pandemic's effect on people's incomes.

Pays off credit card on time

We still have three meals a day but I have to buy lower-quality ingredients.

Regular bank withdrawals

I gamble online but I can afford it.

Multiple daily logging-in to bank app

I can't afford to go out for drinks after work.

Irregular earnings

We manage, just barely.

But underlying this work are some key questions about people's subjective feelings of financial wellbeing. Crucially, what are the potential uses for this kind of research both for regulators and financial firms?

Feelings and facts - when objective and self-reported wellbeing don't align

We believe there is a lot to be learned from situations where objective and self-reported financial wellbeing don't align. Objective measures of financial wellbeing, such as savings and debt balances, are easy to obtain and compare but they are not comprehensive and may not provide a full picture.

A good analogy is measuring prosperity by GDP per capita, which most people agree paints a very incomplete picture of human progress. The Office for National Statistics acknowledged this a few years ago when they began tracking the UK's national wellbeing.

In the realm of personal and household finances, mismatches between how people feel and what we can objectively see about their finances may be crucial. If people are objectively well off, but do not feel that way, then something is amiss.

So we might look at the people who feel more stress than their objective financial situation warrants. Are they in a vulnerable state? Could they be more susceptible to scams and predatory products? Is there anything that firms could do to reassure these people and make them feel more financially secure?

Our research also indicated a correlation (albeit very modest) between online banking activity and subjective feelings of wellbeing. People who log into their mobile banking app regularly report lower financial wellbeing, which may well be linked to the experience of stress. These questions are potentially linked to the relationship between financial wellbeing and mental health, which is increasingly being picked up by industry and policymakers.

And what about people that feel financially well off, even though objectively their finances are not looking good? This could be a coping mechanism, or perhaps a sign of complacency or disengagement. These behaviours could be indicative of broader issues in some parts of the population, such as young people using high-cost short-term credit or putting off saving for their retirement by not engaging with pension products. Put crudely, people with little or no provision for retirement may not be stressed about this fact, but that might simply be because they are not thinking about it.

If people's disengagement with their finances spans across different product areas, then perhaps engaging them in one area could be a 'jump-off point' for greater engagement in other areas.

Greater financial wellbeing through data and technology

Whilst our exploratory analysis sheds some light on the origins of subjective financial wellbeing, we can explain only a small part of the differences between people, and our study does not track differences in wellbeing over time.

Before moving on to questions about offering assistance and designing appropriate communications, there is a need for work with more detailed data. Data science approaches could be used (as the FCA has done previously) to better predict the likelihood of different consumer outcomes, accessing the ever-increasing range of consumer data collected on a daily basis. With greater data sharing through Open Banking and Open Finance, the number and range of parties being able to conduct such research should also increase.

But for data and technology to truly drive greater wellbeing, there are at least a couple of tricky questions that deserve more attention. The first question is around the right blend of subjective/self-reported and objective data. This is because designing new tools and approaches with a focus only on objective data may be quite limiting. The growth of digital channels allows financial institutions to capture subjective measures more regularly and more systematically, which may offer new opportunities.

Capturing subjective metrics may be combined with a conscious opt-in to the use of financial wellbeing tools, which are increasingly being rolled out through digital channels.

Another important issue is the ethical use of data for monitoring subjective financial wellbeing. Although recent research suggests that consumers are largely supportive of banks doing such monitoring, this support may depend on what actions the bank takes based on the data. Banks may have to demonstrate that subjective wellbeing metrics are not used to take advantage of consumers, but rather to help protect and support consumers.

To return to the example of online banking logins, if high rates of logins are a meaningful indicator of possible financial stress, then such data has the potential to be used for both good and ill. This particular correlation in our research is not conclusive, but we believe it illustrates the principle and the potential that data analytics have for monitoring financial wellbeing.

Looking ahead with this in mind, there may be a case for making such wellbeing monitoring explicit and allowing consumers a choice to opt out. There may even be a case for pre-emptive opt-outs for certain consumer groups.

Such questions are obviously closely aligned with wider societal debates on the ethical use of AI.

Studying subjective measures of financial wellbeing is a developing activity, but one that has huge potential. But whatever innovative solutions emerge from such work, ensuring they are welfare-enhancing is a crucial challenge.

26 November 2020

Financial impact of covid-19 already being felt by Britons, especially younger generations

While many Britons have realised that they need to change their financial habits as a result of the coronavirus outbreak, those under 35 are most likely to have felt the pinch so far.

A new Ipsos MORI online survey of 18-75-year olds finds that overall, almost half of Britons (46%) say they have needed to save more money or spend less as a result of the coronavirus outbreak. And it is younger people who are most likely to be resorting to accessing new credit, relying on overdrafts, loans from family and friends or using up savings to avoid the financial pinch.

Overall, 16% say they are using up savings, and another 18% are considering it. But these are much more likely to be younger people – a quarter (25%) of young people say they have already needed to use up their savings, compared with 13% of 35-54s and 11% of 55-75-year olds.

There is a similar story on overdrafts. Overall around one in ten say they have done this (11%), but this rises to 18% of 18-34s, compared with 11% of 35-54s and just 3% of those aged 55-75. And 16% of young people say they have needed to borrow from family or friends, four times more than those aged 35 or older.

In terms of access to more formal finance, 4% of Britons say they have already taken out a loan in response to COVID-19, but this differs significantly by age. Only 1% of those aged between 35 and 75 have done this already while 1 in 10 (11%) of 18-34s say they have. Similarly, 11% of this age group have accessed a new credit card compared with only 2% of 35-54s and not even 1% of 55-75s.

Despite this, 18-34-year olds are also more likely to say they are lending or giving their money to friends and family. Online 8% of Britons overall have done so but almost 1 in 5 (18%) of this younger generation have already done so. Whilst a quarter (26%) of the youngest age group are considering giving their money away compare to just 14% and 15% of 35-54s and 55-75s respectively.

Ben Page, CEO Ipsos MORI, says:

"Despite significant government financial support for businesses and households, we are still starting to see a considerable increase in the debt burden for UK families and this will surely only get more marked if the epidemic continues for many months ."

Technical Note:
Ipsos MORI interviewed a representative sample of 1,072 British adults aged 18-75. Interviews were conducted online: 27th-30th March 2020. Data are weighted to match the profile of the population. All polls are subject to a wide range of potential sources of error.

7 April 2020

Financial measures taken due to the Coronavirus

Thinking about your current financial situation, have you done, or are you considering any of the following due to the coronavirus outbreak? If the statement does not apply to you please say so.

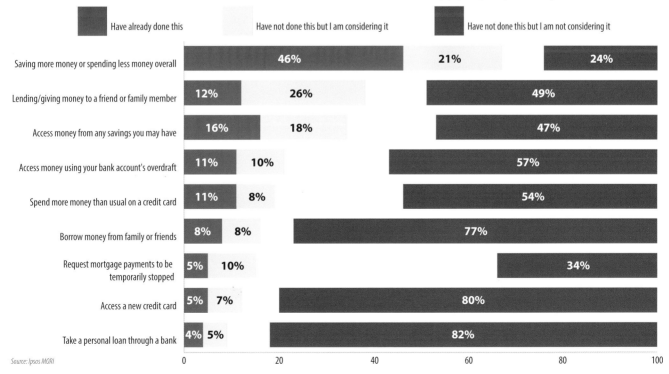

■ Have already done this   □ Have not done this but I am considering it   ■ Have not done this but I am not considering it

	Have already done this	Considering	Not considering
Saving more money or spending less money overall	46%	21%	24%
Lending/giving money to a friend or family member	12%	26%	49%
Access money from any savings you may have	16%	18%	47%
Access money using your bank account's overdraft	11%	10%	57%
Spend more money than usual on a credit card	11%	8%	54%
Borrow money from family or friends	8%	8%	77%
Request mortgage payments to be temporarily stopped	5%	10%	34%
Access a new credit card	5%	7%	80%
Take a personal loan through a bank	4%	5%	82%

Source: Ipsos MORI

Gen Z's dangerous attitude to debt

Easy 'buy now, pay later' apps are facilitating young people's lockdown shopping sprees.

By Eliza Filby

If you want to find out what Generation Z is thinking, look at what's trending on TikTok.

One meme seen millions of times during lockdown has been the #GoHard video, featuring a comedic lip-syncing sketch to the US rapper Kreayshawn's lyrics: "I'd really like to do that but I don't have any f***ing money". The meme reflects the frustrations of wanting to do something and then discovering a genius way to do it without needing to pay. Several of them feature 'buy now, pay later' payment app Klarna as the 'solution'.

Any company would bend over backwards for such authentic, fun — and free — advertising; it reflects the Swedish finance firm Klarna's growing Gen Z-centred customer base. Klarna has been operating in the UK since 2017 and has now linked up with more than 4,500 major retailers from H&M to J.D. Sports. This and other similar apps such as PayPal Credit, Clearpay, and Laybuy enable online customers to either delay or divide the payment across multiple weeks — without incurring interest.

These apps have been godsends for online shoppers during the pandemic because of the way they enable the consumer to purchase several items, try them and send unwanted ones back before they have officially paid for them. Shoppers are not caught up in the inconvenience of delayed reimbursement from retailers. It enables consumers to literally 'try before they buy' even when the shops are all shut.

One TikTok meme sees parcel after parcel pile up on a bed with the tag: "Klarna getting me through lockdown one ASOS package at a time." This trend is real. The price comparison site comparethemarket.com found that 23% of Gen Z have turned to 'buy now, pay later' services during lockdown. While many of us are feeling rather smug about all the savings we are making during this enforced period of restrictive spending, some are experiencing the opposite: online spending sprees funded through delayed payment apps mean that they risk emerging out of lockdown with significant amounts of debt.

"Keep thinking I'm saving money in lockdown and then I remember my FAT klarna bill" tweets one customer. For a large proportion of this generation, whose status emanates from an ever-evolving visual identity through social media, lockdown has been a case of 'you can't change your location but you can change your clothes'. With Klarna the default payment option at the checkout on some sites, it's easy to see why it is so alluring.

As a convenient, flexible alternative to store and credit cards, it appears to be a wholly benign form of debt.

Problems can arise, however, if you miss a payment (which with biweekly instead of the usual monthly payments is all too easy). Klarna itself has estimated that consumers spend on average 55% more when they are given the option of delaying or paying over several weeks (without admitting that this may be money customers do not have). Email and text reminders are sent, but the account will be sent to a debt collection agency when customers fail to act. Klarna has said that it has clear T&Cs, a strict vetting process and responsive customer service but an investigation by The Daily Telegraph found that 30,000 customers have already had their credit damaged because of missed payments.

As debt services go, it would be wrong to put them in the same class as Wonga or BrightHouse (which, incidentally, folded during lockdown) but we are right to question their corporate responsibility when this service is so quick, easy and marketed chiefly at the young. With its millennial pink logo and its focus on social media influencers such as Love Island contestants, Klarna has successfully tapped into a tricky market that can often allude major retailers. Its recent campaign "Shop like a Queen" was a deliberate appeal to the LGBTQI community, sponsoring the former Ru Paul's US Drag Race stars Katya Zamolodchikova and Trixie Mattel's YouTube show UNHhhh.

But a generation that has had a smartphone in their palm since their early teens is wary of crude endorsements. One US viewer complained on Reddit that he was 'disappointed' to see UNHhhh "turn into an extended commercial for [a] credit scheme". This generation, which grew up in the wake of the 2008 financial crash, also takes a sceptical view of investments, the stock market and established money lenders. According to the consultancy firm Cassandra, only 34% of Gen Z trust banks.

Gen Z are wired differently to millennials when it comes to consumption, debt and saving. Whereas millennials grew up in the boom years, Gen Z's childhood (when your attitudes towards money are formulated) was defined by the crash, followed by austerity and sluggish recovery in the wake of the Brexit referendum. They watched their parents struggle and will now themselves experience the Corona Crash. They won't able to rely on the bank of Mum and Dad in the same way that a significant number of millennials did.

They also grew up during the fintech revolution, during which automated payments and cashless transactions became the new normal, and the weight of coins in your pocket was an alien sensation. Add to that the era of fast-fashion, fast-consumption and you have a generation that is on the one hand much more prudent than millennials in valuing money, but also much more vulnerable when it comes to spending it.

The combination of tech and tough times has made them more resourceful and more entrepreneurial — a number generate their own money from a younger age. They are also savvy shoppers to whom price comparison is second nature, while their ethical credentials and fashion-conscious aesthetic has triggered a revolution in the second-hand clothes market which rivals that of fast-fashion. Depop, a buying and selling app, has experienced a 90% increase in traffic since 1 April.

There are signs that they are more inclined to save than millennials too. When HSBC ran a survey asking Gen Z and millennials what they would do with £1,000 cash, 72% of Gen Z (compared with 55% of millennials) said they would put it into a savings account. The challenger bank Monzo, an app-only bank whose card is now a staple in every Gen Z wallet, catered for the new banking priorities of young people post-Crash who wanted greater control over their finances through its spending notifications and saving pot features. It also recently signed a deal with the saving app Emma, which it plans to launch for those as young as 11.

Generation Z may see the benefits of saving, but they also have a more relaxed attitude towards spending and debt. Student loans have normalised debt for the young but not given them the skills to manage it. Debt, of any kind, has been made to feel inconsequential. As one commented on TikTok responding to a #GoHard Klarna video:

"I have a debt collection agency after me for a £15 ASOS order" — complete with a laughing emoji. The social shame of living on the never-never, common up until the 1980s, is not something that bothers this generation.

Nor perhaps does the prospect of insolvency. Bankruptcy claims among the young have increased tenfold in three years: under-25s now account for 6.5% of all cases, according to the accountancy firm RSM. One debt advice company estimated that this demographic represented 14% of all clients in 2018, with an average debt of £6,000. A study found that 18% of 18-24-year-olds use their credit card for bills and essentials.

The success of these apps also lies in the fact that Generation Z, more than any other generation, has been conditioned to the 'one-click' transaction. Apps such as Klarna do not just encourage the "I want it now" urge but also normalise the frictionless buying experience. This was pioneered by Amazon and Apple but in the case of Klarna, is financed through debt.

The move to a cashless society has meant that all ages have experienced a growing detachment and responsibility from the transaction — the psychological difference between a couple of clicks online and physically handing over cash. This becomes problematic when it is a debt-based transaction by someone young, financially vulnerable, used to one-click credit and with an easy attitude towards debt. Parents have been talking to their kids about the perilous nature of social interactions online; it could be that they also need to start educating them on the perilous nature of financial transactions online too.

But beware lecturing the young on money. The days of delayed gratification are long gone for most of us. Generation Z are no more consumerist than their parents, and certainly more financially inventive, informed and resourceful than millennials. Some responsibility must lie with companies themselves in providing full transparency of terms, thorough checks on vulnerable customers and a genuine commitment to responsible debt control. The debt industry will always work out new methods to lure consumers and for the majority, debt is convenient and, if managed, perfectly sound financial behaviour. But we are facing a fierce financial headwind that has already disproportionately impacted the young.

One bruised Klarna customer on Reddit offered a solution: "Saving seems to be an act of resistance." To Gen Z, a savvy, activist generation, recalibrating shrewd financial behaviour into a political act might just gain traction.

10 June 2020

Is all debt bad? Good debt vs. bad debt

By Nigel Woollsey

At a glance

- Not all debt is bad – some assets and benefits are a good investment in your financial future.
- Avoid using credit to buy 'non-essential' items or services, unless you can pay off the whole amount before any interest is charged.
- Good debt doesn't mean that the asset purchased necessarily increases in value, so long as it has additional benefits over time, such as a car loan.

Why not all debt is 'bad'

Very often people will assume that all debt is 'bad'. Sometimes owing money or obtaining any form of credit is considered indicative of poor money management skills. However, this is simply not true. Debt and credit can serve very useful and positive functions. Used correctly and with care, the use of credit and even debt can be 'good'.

Examples of good debt

Good debt is a planned and budgeted for investment in your financial future. Sometimes having a small debt now can prevent a much larger expenditure later. Good credit can be used to purchase assets that can depreciate only very slowly or in some instances grow to be worth more in time.

Mortgage

Investing in bricks and mortar has long been the long-term investment of choice for many. For most people, they can look forward to their home increasing in value over the course of several years. Of course, short-term fluctuations in the housing market might see your home drop in price temporarily, but over the longer-term you are likely to make a profit. In addition, mortgage interest rates tend to be lower than many other types of credit.

Car or other vehicle loan

An affordable car (or other vehicle) purchased with credit is a good example of an asset that provides a good, long-term return for your debt. Of course, cars, vans and other vehicles do typically go down in value over time, so the benefit is not in its resale value, but rather in the practical benefits of having a reliable means of transport – especially if this is required for work or your own business.

However, there comes a point where a car loan can become a 'bad' debt – for example, spending a lot more to purchase a new or luxury vehicle where an affordable alternative will do just as well. Buying a brand-new Rolls Royce for a commute trip to your workplace of just 10 min is a rather extreme but illustrative example.

Student loan

This is a good form of debt where you are investing in your own future employment prospects. For many, a University degree or college education enables them to reap the rewards of a higher-paying job with better career prospects. Of course, this does mean starting out your career with

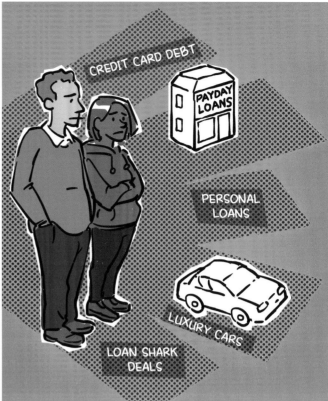

large debt, but this is offset by the low interest rates and the fact that you will not be required to repay this until you are earning a certain amount.

Credit building debt

It's an unfortunate truth that in order to get a good credit score (or repair a bad one) you must first get credit in some form. Younger people who are looking to access credit for the first time will find that they are considered a 'bad' risk.

This is not because they have demonstrated poor money management skills, but rather the lender has nothing to base their assessment on as to how they will deal with credit.

For these people (and those rebuilding a credit history), having debt that you are actively repaying, on time and with no problems, is a good thing and works to improve their financial standing.

Business loans

In the case of business, loans that help the business grow and prosper are a positive use of credit. This is especially true if the business succeeds and becomes much more valuable as a result.

Bad debt examples

Bad debt adds little or nothing at all to your overall assets or prospects. This is the money paid for items that decrease in value quickly or may have no value at all after the initial purchase.

Credit card debts

Unless you are wisely using a 0% interest purchase credit card, items that are bought using a credit card come with relatively high interest rates. If you don't pay off the whole amount every month, the money owed in interest can quickly outstrip the value of the asset purchased.

This becomes even worse if you are using a credit card for purchasing things like restaurant meals or holidays. These are things that leave you with no discernible assets (beyond sheer enjoyment) and consequently can be seen as 'bad'.

Payday loans

It's hard to imagine a form of credit that makes you pay so much for so little. These short-term loans are intended for small amounts taken out over less than 30 days. With interest rates that can be around 1000% p.a., these can quickly escalate to be a highly expensive way of using credit.

Borrowing money to service other debts

Using credit to service the repayments on another debt is an excellent example of 'bad' debt. For example, using a cash advance from one credit card to pay off the minimum amount on another does nothing to resolve the original debt and will result in high interest rates and even more fees to be paid on the cash advance.

Moneyfacts tip

Where possible, avoid using credit to pay for assets that depreciate in value very quickly (such as clothes, meals out and luxury holidays) and when you cannot repay the total borrowed in less than a month.

21 January 2021

What does the future of money look like?

Digital currencies, payments, the cashless society – the world of money is changing. Naresh Aggarwal looks at some emerging scenarios.

By Naresh Aggarwal

Over the past few years, I've come across a number of reports on the future of the financial markets exploring what the changing dynamics might mean for businesses, citizens, regulators and governments.

The Bank of England's Future of Finance report from September last year, for example, is a comprehensive exploration of the forces shaping the economy and what that means for the world of finance.

Others use personas to tell a story. Swiss payments company SIX, for instance, has recently published a 50-page white paper. In it, you can follow the antics of Felix, whose interactions take place largely in the digital space. The paper itself is well worth a read, but if you don't have the time, my personal observations follow.

The report considers seven different futures that would impact the cash infrastructure and service space, and ranks them according to likelihood. These scenarios all have profound impacts for the treasurer and, even if some seem unlikely, the paper gives a sense of what the future may look like.

1. Digital rules

Digital payments have substantially increased in convenience compared with cash as digital-user interfaces expand into ever-more human activities.

Cash as a means of payment falls by 40-70%, as people demand immediacy in everything they do. At the same time, cash continues to be perceived and widely used as a store of value.

2. Digital currency

Cash holdings have dropped by 80% as cash is no longer the dominant means of payment, and digital money and assets have increasingly displaced cash as a safe store of value.

Cash may continue to be used as a means of payment by the non-digitally inclined and by digitally savvy people for self-regulation, for its tangibility, for teaching the value of money and out of security and privacy concerns.

Some people continue to maintain cash holdings as a back-up means of payment for 'blackouts' or times when networks are interrupted.

3. Rise of the central bank digital currency

Anyone can hold digital currency issued by the central bank – referred to as central bank digital currency. People can choose where to hold their digital currencies – in an account with the central bank or a commercial bank.

They may continue to use commercial banks to hold their digital currency and assume the counterparty risk in exchange for a higher interest on their deposits.

4. Central banks are dead – long live central banks!

New, centrally issued currencies are the new money; new currencies and issuers replace sovereign currencies and central banks. Traditional central banks, such as the US Federal Reserve or the European Central Bank, first become irrelevant – and then disappear.

Non-sovereign currencies become the dominant form of money. These currencies are not pegged to a sovereign currency or basket, but are under the full control of their issuers. Examples include Libra, M-Pesa and Tencent's QQ coin.

5. A cashless world is born

Cash disappears completely as governments withdraw it to reduce criminal activity and tax evasion.

A digital cash infrastructure may take the place of the physical cash infrastructure, which guarantees the same levels of security and anonymity or privacy as physical cash. There is no cash flowing through the economy any more.

Central banks can more easily impose deep negative interest rates on digital money deposits to further economic activity, by reducing incentives to save in order to increase aggregate consumption/demand.

6. Moneyless begins

There is no such thing as money anymore and no consensus on an asset as a medium of exchange, store of value or unit of account.

Different people use different assets (or sets of assets) as a store of value and as their unit of account, 'paying' with assets ranging from 'usage rights to their data' to 'usage rights to their apartment', financial instruments they own (such as equity or debt securities) and sovereign currencies.

Employees can ask to be paid directly in those assets that they prefer as a store of value.

7. It's a bitcoin world

Cryptocurrencies (such as Bitcoin and Ether) have replaced central-bank-issued currencies as the dominant forms of money. Crypto-contracts are the dominant form of contracts.

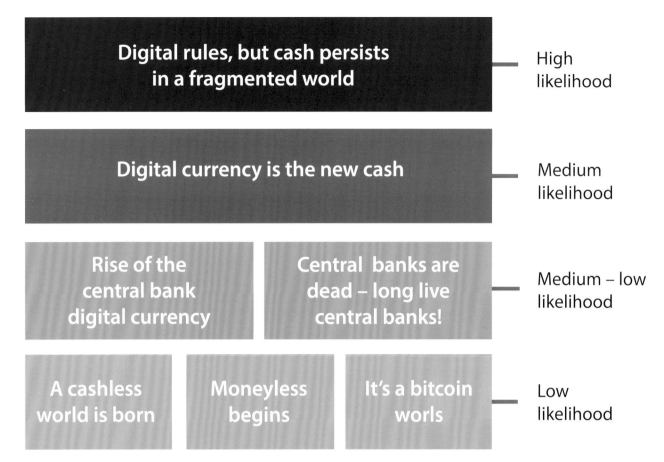

Digital rules, but cash persists in a fragmented world	High likelihood
Digital currency is the new cash	Medium likelihood
Rise of the central bank digital currency / **Central banks are dead – long live central banks!**	Medium – low likelihood
A cashless world is born / **Moneyless begins** / **It's a bitcoin worls**	Low likelihood

Digital services take the form of open-source code stored on these permission-less distributed ledgers and decentrally executed by participants to these ledgers, which are known as decentralised applications, or DApps.

My reflections

How likely are these scenarios? We already see elements of many of them operating in practice or as trials. We see debates about the value of cash and the changing economic models for ATM machines.

Central bank digital currencies are appearing more frequently in the news, with a recent report from the European Central Bank titled 'Exploring anonymity in central bank digital currencies' and an announcement from the Peoples Bank of China that its digital currency "can now be said to be ready".

Whichever scenario or hybrid we end up with, citizens and businesses will need to consider three, key factors:

Trust/data All of these scenarios require digital identities and authorisations to be more accessible and trusted both by all parties to payments. As payment institutions open traditionally closed interfaces to their digital vaults, and customer data to third parties to seamlessly connect their digital apps (for example, digital wallets), regulators and users will need to increase their trust over access to their data.

Cyber The growing reliance on non-physical payment activity and the use of the cloud will increase cyber risks. As threats continue to increase in sophistication, secure data communication may require a rebuild of the underlying internet architecture/protocol.

Convenience As we provide more seamless access to a digital world, how do we ensure that no one is left behind?

Can everyone handle frictionless payment activity? Concerns have already arisen over the growth of the buy now pay later retail shopping model.

Conclusion

The debate over the use of cash and digital will continue to evolve over the coming decade (as it has over the past one).

Policymakers and regulators will need to make sure that any changes reflect the needs of both the technically savvy as well as those less comfortable or able to access digital services.

Even if not payment champions, treasurers will need to stay abreast of these developments to make sure their businesses and their liquidity management processes continue to be fit for purpose.

This means being able to assess the impact of developments in the payments space and recognising when some may be detrimental.

The policy and technical team are active participants in working groups run by the Bank of England and pay.uk, and welcome any concerns that treasurers may have over proposed changes to the UK payment landscape.

12 February 2020

About the author: Naresh Aggarwal is associate director, policy and technical, at The Association of Corporate Treasurers

Spotlight on digital currency with MyBnk

What's a digital currency?

It's a type of money that's only available in a digital or electronic form. You can't feel it or touch it like cash and it's usually stored in an e-wallet like an app or computer programme. It's also encrypted, which means it's one of the most secure, anonymous forms of monetary transaction there is. Whilst it is secure, as we are not financial advisors, we are educators, so we strongly suggest not getting involved in digital currency until you are over 18 and have done extensive research of your own to find out what's best for you.

An early use of Bitcoin was for fast food. In 2010 Programmer Laszlo Hanyecz traded 10,000 bitcoins for two Papa John's pizzas – about $41 at the time. Today that order would have cost nearly £400 million.

What's bitcoin?

It's one of the first and most popular digital currencies on the market, but it's not the only one. You may have heard of Ethereum, Litecoin and DogeCoin. There are literally thousands of them!

What's the blockchain?

Blockchain is a database used to track transactions. Since digital currency doesn't have physical cash or bank accounts, the blockchain ensures digital coins are where they should be. Think of it as a list of all the transactions ever made by all the people using that currency. Records are public, meaning anyone can see it and it can't be edited.

This data could be someone spending, mining or selling digital coins. As new data comes in, it is entered into a new 'block'. Once the block is filled with data it is 'chained' onto the previous block, which links data together in chronological order. Most are 'decentralised' meaning no one person or organisation holds all the records, like a bank or government.

How can I get some?

There are two ways: buy it or mine it. You'll also need an e-wallet - there are lots out there and not all are tied to a currency.

What is buying?

Right now a single Bitcoin costs about £40,000. It's essentially an investment and involves a lot of risk, meaning you are not guaranteed to make a profit and could lose what you've put in.

Remember, digital currencies have no intrinsic value (like a house for example), it's just a bunch of 1's and 0's that people have DECIDED are worth something. Prices go up and down

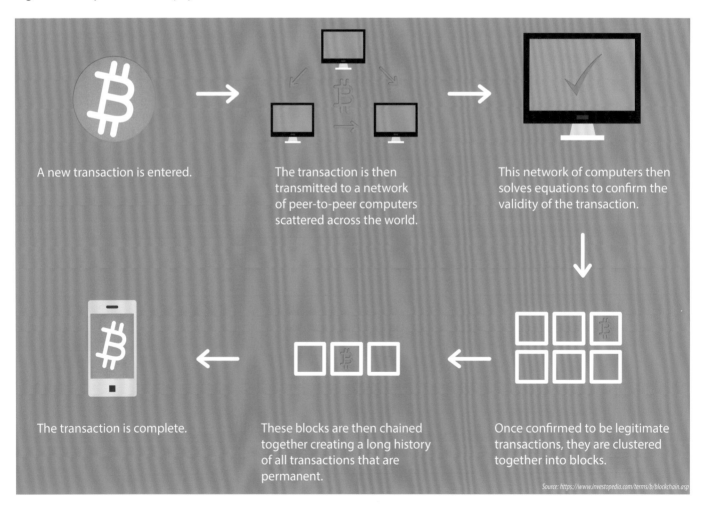

A new transaction is entered.

The transaction is then transmitted to a network of peer-to-peer computers scattered across the world.

This network of computers then solves equations to confirm the validity of the transaction.

The transaction is complete.

These blocks are then chained together creating a long history of all transactions that are permanent.

Once confirmed to be legitimate transactions, they are clustered together into blocks.

Source: https://www.investopedia.com/terms/b/blockchain.asp

– if you buy a Bitcoin today for £40,000 and tomorrow the price shoots up to £50,000, then you've made a cool profit… IF you sell. But there is every chance that tomorrow that coin could be worth £5,000 – and selling then means a huge loss.

A few years ago, a lot of people got excited about Bitcoin pushing the price from about £4,000 to £20,000. After the initial gain it dropped back to under £10,000 and has been going mostly up since. Investing now means spending a lot of money in a volatile market. The increase could be down to more people and businesses accepting it as payment or a loss of faith in traditional currencies, which can be manipulated by banks and governments.

What is mining?

Mining for digital coins involves using a computer to work out complex maths problems. Sometimes, this will include doing the background work to ensure the blockchain is up to date. Once complete, everyone involved in mining that coin will get a cut of it, usually based on how much they contributed.

Sounds great right? Just leave your PC on and make money? Unfortunately, once a coin is mined, the next one becomes harder to get and so on. It takes more time, power and people to mine a coin meaning you need to share it with more people. In fact, most will need to spend thousands of pounds on graphics cards to make a 'mining rig' to do it effectively.

Heard of mining pools? These are groups who 'jump in' and pay a website to 'mine' on your behalf using the limited power of your PC – the site usually takes a cut of your profits. You're relying on the organiser to ensure it's fair, and some pools have been shown to be scams, so you need to be very careful.

How do you actually use digital currency?

You can sell it on markets like a stock or share, minus a fee. This releases your digital currency into cash that you can move to a bank account.

You can pay for things directly. Microsoft, Burger King, KFC and Tesla all offer the ability to pay with Bitcoin. You will struggle to use it on the high street, but some online retailers, like Amazon, may accept it soon.

There are some products being planned like the physical metal Crypto.com Visa card which lets you use your cryptocurrency as a debit card to use in shops. The shop receives payment in pounds but Crypto.com will take some of your cryptocurrency and convert it for the sale – you just hand over the card like normal. It's unpredictable exactly what items will cost and the value fluctuates. It will likely cost if you want to get the most benefit from systems like this so make sure you understand the full costs before signing up to products or services.

Finally, Bitcoin ATMs – you can literally buy and sell Bitcoin at kiosks all over the country now, but fees and charges are a downside.

Safety and security

Bitcoin was originally created to keep money safe. However, as with anything digital, people have found ways to crack codes and scam people out of their money.

As long as you keep your e-wallet details safe only you can access your Bitcoin.

However, if you lose your password or code there is no way to recover them. You can't withdraw it and put in a piggy bank, it HAS to be stored digitally.

One Welsh man found out the hard way that you need to keep all your wallets safe. After mining 7,500 Bitcoins he threw away his laptop, leaving his e-wallet on the hard drive. Those coins are now worth £300 MILLION. The council turned down £50m so he could hunt the tip.

And it's not just wallets you need to keep safe, you need the passwords too. Stefan Thomas has around £280m in Bitcoin in his wallet…but has forgotten the password and only has one attempt left before it's locked forever.

Scammers will try to get you to send Bitcoins or phish your deets. Internet fraudsters use digital currencies as a payment method due to its untraceable nature. The usual rule of 'if it's too good to be true…' definitely applies.

23 April 2021

Bitcoin isn't getting greener: four environmental myths about cryptocurrency debunked

THE CONVERSATION

An article from The Conversation.

By Peter Howson Senior Lecturer in International Development, Northumbria University

The price of bitcoin has reached US$50,000 (£36,095) – another all-time high. It's hard to believe that 10,000 bitcoin would only buy a couple of pizzas ten years ago. It's even stranger to think that bitcoins are completely virtual. You can't hold one, except on a hard drive, and there's no underlying asset to them. A bitcoin is simply a digital representation of the computer power needed to make one, what's called its "proof-of-work".

This isn't actually a new idea though. Rai stones were one of the first forms of money used on the Micronesian islands of Yap. To get hold of a Rai, you had to row a canoe for 500km or so to Palau and chisel away at some local limestone. Then you needed to take the 3m-wide lump of rock back to Yap without sinking in the Pacific. No one is quite sure when it started, but the practice is at least several centuries old. Yapese money had no inherent value. For everyone to respect the proof-of-work, the process was deliberately inefficient and incredibly resource-intensive, just like bitcoin.

Instead of relying on intrepid voyagers, bitcoin uses a global network of competing computers. Like safe crackers at a safe-cracking contest, these bitcoin mining machines guess the combination to a digital lock (a long string of digits) with the correct combination winning a few new bitcoins. The combination changes every ten minutes, and the contest continues.

This might all sound like a harmless game of digital bingo. But with more and more people enticed by the heady rewards, bitcoin mining on some days uses as much energy as Poland and generates 37 million tonnes of CO_2 each year.

New institutional investors, like the carmaker, Tesla, are driving the asset's price skywards while ignoring bitcoin's climate-changing appetite. And to keep the bull market charging, supporters are working hard to argue for bitcoin's green credentials.

For the sake of a stable climate, these myths need debunking.

Myth one: bitcoin mining is becoming more efficient

Bitcoin's carbon emissions are not the network's only dirty secret. In 2011, competing miners could win the bitcoin bingo with an average laptop. Today, viable operations

require investing in warehouses filled with specialised hardware known as Application Specific Integrated Circuits (ASIC). As the majority of mining costs come from energy to run these units, bitcoin miners are always careful to use the cheapest. To avoid wasting energy, the global arms race for bitcoin requires ASICs to be replaced for newer and more efficient models every year.

ASICs can't be easily repurposed for general computing. Redundant units create around 11,500 tonnes of hazardous electronic waste each year, much of which is dumped on cities in the global south.

Myth two: bitcoin encourages investment in clean energy

Chinese hydroelectric power plants are popular spots for bitcoin mining. While China cracks down on the industry, 61% of bitcoin mining is powered by fossil fuels.

Cheap coal in Australia has found new buyers through bitcoin, as formerly redundant coal mines are reopened to power mining. Miners are willing to move anywhere for residual energy, increasing the profitability of natural gas in Siberia and supporting oil drilling in Texas.

In Virunga National Park in the Democratic Republic of Congo, bitcoin miners are getting special access to cheap, clean energy produced by an EU-funded hydroelectric plant. The plant was designed to help locals find livelihoods beyond poaching and stop them resorting to scouring parkland for wood fuel. Bitcoin miners employ armies of computer servers, not the ex-combatants the plant could help.

Myth three: bitcoin replaces the need for gold mining

Gold mining is one of the world's most destructive industries. Bitcoin was originally intended as a digital replacement for gold that was also a deflationary means of exchange, capable of rendering wasteful banks and regulators redundant.

But for many institutional investors, gold is being bought to hedge against bitcoin's volatility. Tesla poured US$1.5 billion into bitcoin, but also declared an interest in gold. While bitcoin is currently experiencing all-time price highs, gold hit one of its own in 2020.

Nor has bitcoin displaced traditional finance institutions. Major banks are vying to get very rich indeed on the back of it.

Myth four: corporate players will boost market for 'green bitcoin'

Some argue that institutional investors can turn bitcoin green. Yves Bennaim, the founder of Swiss cryptocurrency think tank 2B4CH, claims that as investors like Tesla push prices up, "there will be more incentive to make investments in renewable sources of energy" for bitcoin mining. But miners will always use the cheapest option to maximise returns. It's not possible to allocate additional rewards to miners using renewables, because it's difficult to know exactly which bitcoin miners use renewables.

Unfortunately, there is currently no such thing as a "green bitcoin".

Not all cryptocurrencies are as energy-intensive as bitcoin, though. There are alternatives to proof-of-work. The second biggest blockchain project, ethereum, is switching to proof-of-stake, a new system which is supposed to remove the need for data miners and perpetual hardware updates. Bitcoins are dirty things, but pointing this out to would-be investors should not mean throwing the blockchain baby out with bitcoin's bath water.

17 February 2021

British gamblers more likely than public to use cryptocurrencies, but scepticism remains

By Oliver Rowe, DIrector of Reputation Research

With each passing year, decentralized cryptocurrencies like Bitcoin are integrating further into the modern financial system, and the gambling sector is no exception. As the industry entrenches itself more deeply into digital behaviours, it's important to understand the attitudes gamblers in Britain hold about digital money.

Among those British adults who gamble online at least once a month, 17% say they are likely to use some form of cryptocurrency in the next 12 months, according to YouGov data, which is considerably more than the 11% of British adults in general.

However, there remains a lack of understanding of the concept of cryptocurrency among some punters. While 74% of the general public say they don't really understand cryptocurrency, that number inches slightly higher among regular online gamblers at 75%.

This dearth of knowledge may be feeding scepticism. For instance, more than half (54%) of the nation's regular punters say cryptocurrencies are not to be trusted, and again that's a slightly higher rate than the general public (52%).

Further, 52% of gamblers think blockchain-backed cryptos like Bitcoin are just a passing fad. Once again, that feeling is more pervasive among those who gamble than the general public.

With all that said, it may seem as though crypto will be a tougher sell for gamblers.

However, comfort and understanding around it is significantly higher among younger gamblers, even when we compare the group to Britain's non-gambling Millennial population. A third of Millennial gamblers say cryptocurrencies are the future of online financial transactions and 13% say they're willing to give up their bank account and use crypto instead.

There are many reasons for the industry and consumers to be excited about this new chapter in currency. Right now, banks don't have authority of virtual funds, which means the consumer doesn't have to pay transaction fees on withdrawals or deposits. What's more, neither the operators nor the users have to worry about exchange rates. Because they are a decentralized asset, there is no need to go through traditional approval channels, meaning transactions are faster than traditional currency transfers.

Looking at the cryptocurrency landscape in general at the moment, it's still dominated by Bitcoin. Nearly one in seven British adults have used the digital currency in the last year.

About a quarter have used Etherium (24%) and 18% have used Binance coin.

Holding cryptocurrency right now isn't for the faint of heart as digital coins are unregulated and highly speculative. The price of Bitcoin, for example, hit US$60,000 in March before dropping below US$55,000 just days later.

But regular gamblers have a higher tolerance for risk than the general public. For one, this group is more likely to say they like to take risks in the stock market (17% vs. 12% of the general population) and that's truer still among younger punters (25%).

Crypto is making its way into the mainstream in significant ways and those not offering Bitcoin transactions may want to reconsider in the future. Large established financial brands like Mastercard and PayPal have recently announced intentions to accept cryptocurrency, lending further legitimacy to the concept of digital currency.

Over the next few years, it's crucial for the industry to track how widespread crypto usage will become and understand their customer's relationship with decentralized money to ensure they're offering the payment options their market prefers.

17 May 2021

The pros and cons of moving to a cashless society

By Justin Pritchard

A cashless society might sound like something out of science fiction, but it's already on its way. Several powerful forces are behind the move to a cash-free world, including some governments and large financial services companies.[1][2]

However, no society has gone totally cash-free just yet. In addition to logistical challenges, several social issues need to be addressed before society can give up on cash entirely. The benefits and disadvantages below can give you an idea of the myriad of effects going cashless can have on money and banking as you know it.

Benefits of a cashless society

Those with the technological ability to take advantage of a cashless society will likely find that it's more convenient. As long as you have your card or phone, you have instantaneous access to all your cash holdings. Convenience isn't the only benefit. Here are some other benefits.

Lower crime rates

Carrying cash makes you an easy target for criminals. Once the money is taken from your wallet and put into a criminal's wallet, it'll be difficult to track that cash or prove that it's yours. One study by American and German researchers found that crime in Missouri dropped by 9.8% as the state replaced cash welfare benefits with Electronic Benefit Transfer (EBT) cards.[3]

Automatic paper trails

Similarly, financial crime should also dry up in a cashless society. Illegal transactions, such as illegal gambling or drug operations, typically use cash so that there isn't a record of the transaction and the money is easier to launder. Money laundering becomes much harder if the source of funds is always clearly identifiable. It is harder to hide income and evade taxes when there's a record of every payment you receive.

Cash management costs money

Going cashless isn't just convenient. It costs money to print bills and coins. Businesses need to store the money, get more when they run out, deposit cash when they have too much on hand, and in some cases, hire companies to transport cash safely. Banks hire large security teams to protect branches against physical banks' robberies. Spending time and resources moving money around and protecting large sums of cash could become a thing of the past in a cashless future.

International payments become much easier

When you travel, you may need to exchange your dollars for local currency. However, if you're traveling in a country that accepts cashless transactions, you don't need to worry about exchange rates or how much of the local currency you'll need to withdraw. Instead, your mobile device handles everything for you.

Disadvantages of a cash-free world

Depending on your perspective, going cashless might actually be more problematic than beneficial. Here are some of the major downsides associated with a cashless financial system.

Digital transactions sacrifice privacy

Electronic payments aren't as private as cash payments. You might trust the organizations that handle your data, and you might have nothing to hide. However, the more information you have floating around online, the more likely it is to wind up in malicious hands. Cash allows you to spend money and receive funds anonymously.

Cashless transactions are exposed to hacking risks

Hackers are the bank robbers and muggers of the electronic world. In a cashless society, you're more exposed to hackers. If you are targeted, and somebody drains your account, you may not have any alternative ways to spend money. Even if you're protected under federal law, it will still be inconvenient to restore your financial standing after a breach.

Technology problems could impact your access to funds

Glitches, outages, and innocent mistakes can also cause problems, leaving you without the ability to buy things when you need to. Likewise, merchants have no way to accept payments when systems malfunction. Even something as simple as a dead phone battery could leave you "penniless," in a sense.

Economic inequality could become exacerbated

Unless special outreach efforts are made, the poor and unbanked will likely have an even harder time in a cashless society. If smartphone purchases become the standard way to transact, for example, those who can't afford smartphones will be left behind. The U.K. is experimenting with contactless ways to donate to charities and homeless individuals, but these efforts may not be developed enough yet to substitute cash donations.[4]

Payment providers could charge fees

If society is forced to choose from just a few payment methods, or if one app becomes the standard payment

app, the companies who develop these services may not offer them for free. Payment processors may cash in on the high volumes by imposing fees, eliminating the savings that should come from less cash handling.

The temptation to overspend may increase

When you spend with cash, you recognize the financial impact by physically taking the cash out of your pocket and giving it to someone else. With electronic payments, on the other hand, it's easy to swipe, tap, or click without noticing how much you spend. Consumers may have to rethink the ways they manage their spending.

Negative interest rates could be passed onto customers

When all money is electronic, negative interest rates could have a more direct effect on consumers. Countries like Denmark, Japan, and Switzerland have already experimented with negative interest rates.[5]

Note: Dropping the interest rate is typically a move to stimulate an economy, but the result is that money loses purchasing power.[6]

According to the International Monetary Fund, negative interest rates reduce bank profitability, and banks could be tempted to hike fees on customers to make up that deficit. In 2020, banks are limited in their ability to pass on those costs because customers can simply withdraw their cash from the bank if they don't like the fees. In the future, if customers can't withdraw cash from the bank, they may have to accept any additional fees.

What does a cashless society look like?

Without cash, payments happen electronically. Instead of using paper and coins to exchange value, you authorize a transfer of funds from a bank account to another person or business. The logistics are still developing, but there are some hints as to how a cashless society might evolve.

Credit and debit cards are among the most popular cash alternatives in use today. Cards alone may not be enough to support a 100% cashless society. Mobile devices may instead become a primary tool for payments.

Electronic payment apps, like Zelle, PayPal, and Venmo, are helpful for person-to-person payments (P2P payments). In addition, bill-splitting apps allow friends to split their bills easily and in a fair manner. Fintech companies like Stripe, Adyen, and Fiserv support business-to-consumer (B2C), business-to-business (B2B), or what they now merge into account-to-account (A2A) online payments in a reliable and speedy fashion.

Mobile payment services and mobile wallets like Apple Pay provide secure, cash-free payments. Many nations that use cash sparingly have already seen mobile devices become a common tool for payments.

Cryptocurrencies are also part of the discussion. They're already used for money transfers, and they introduce competition and innovation that may help keep costs low. However, there are risks and regulatory hurdles that make them impractical for most consumers, so they might not be ready for widespread use, yet.

Examples of cashless societies

Several nations are already making moves to eliminate cash, with the push coming from both consumers and government bodies. Sweden and India are two notable examples, with two different outcomes.

Sweden

It's not uncommon to see signs that say "No Cash Accepted" in Swedish shops. According to the European Payments Council, cash transactions accounted for just 1% of Sweden's GDP in 2019, and cash withdrawals have been steadily declining by about 10% a year.[2] Consumers are mostly happy with this situation, but those who struggle to keep up with technological developments continue to rely on cash. Sweden is gearing up to become the first cashless nation in the world, with an economy 100 percent digital by 2023.

India

The Indian government banned 500 and 1,000 rupee notes in November 2016, in an effort to penalize criminals and those working in the informal economy.[1] The implementation was controversial, in part because roughly 99% of those banknotes were eventually deposited.[7] The fact that the banknotes were deposited means criminals weren't punished for hoarding untraceable cash, which had been the intent of the move. The Economic Times cited the Reserve Bank of India as it reported that electronic transactions increased temporarily, but cash returned to pre-demonetization levels by the end of 2017.[8]

Note: While these two examples had varying levels of success, both countries struggled to address how the marginalized will fare in a 100% cashless society.

1. British Broadcasting Corporation. "India Scraps 500 and 1,000 Rupee Bank Notes Overnight." Accessed June 10, 2020.

2. European Payments Council. "Sweden: Cashless Society and Digital Transformation." Accessed June 10, 2020.

3. IZA: Institute of Labor Economics. "Less Cash, Less Crime: Evidence From the Electronic Benefit Transfer Program," Page 2. Accessed June 10, 2020.

4. The Guardian. "'Sorry, I've Only Got My Card': Can the Homeless Adapt to Cashless Society?" Accessed June 10, 2020.

5. International Monetary Fund. "Back to Basics: How Can Interest Rates Be Negative?" Accessed June 10, 2020.

6. Wells Fargo. "Q&A on Negative Interest Rates." Accessed June 10, 2020.

7. British Broadcasting Corporation. "India Rupee: Illegal Cash Crackdown Failed – Bank Report." Accessed June 10, 2020.

8. The Economic Times. "A Year After Note Ban, Cashless Economy Is Still a Distant Dream." Accessed June 10, 2020.

30 April 2021

Key Facts

- Some anthropologists say the earliest historical evidence of something similar to what we call money emerged around 5000 years ago in Mesopotamia (modern-day Iraq). (page 2)

- Banks make sure your money is kept safe and have served this role since ancient Greek and Roman times. (page 3)

- Over 9 in 10 adults make payments using a debit card at least once a month. (page 3)

- The original meaning of 'bank' comes from the Old High German word meaning 'bench'. Early bankers in Europe used benches as makeshift counters for banking transactions. (page 3)

- The first recorded use of 'paper' money was in China in the seventh century. (page 4)

- The Bank of England was established in 1694 to raise money for King William III's war effort. (page 4)

- In 1853 the first fully printed banknotes were introduced. (page 4)

- 94% of UK parents believe it is a school's role to provide financial education. (page 5)

- 66% of parents choose to give a regular allowance. (page 10)

- A survey of 2,000 parents found 12 per cent had experienced their pre-school children spending money online. (page 13)

- Data released by the Gambling Commission in 2019 revealed eleven to 16-year-olds who admitted to gambling said they spent £17 per week on games, such as fruit machines and online "loot boxes", equalling half of their weekly allowance of £34. (page 14)

- Research shows that 78% of students worry about making ends meet. (page 16)

- The Office for National Statistics (ONS) said the public sector had borrowed more in February 2021 than during any other February since records began in 1993. (page 20)

- An Ipsos MORI online survey of 18-75-year olds found that overall, almost half of Britons (46%) said they have needed to save more money or spend less as a result of the coronavirus outbreak. (page 25)

- When HSBC ran a survey asking Gen Z and millennials what they would do with £1,000 cash, 72% of Gen Z (compared with 55% of millennials) said they would put it into a savings account. (page 27)

- An early use of Bitcoin was for fast food. In 2010 Programmer Laszlo Hanyecz traded 10,000 bitcoins for two Papa John's pizzas – about $41 at the time. Today that order would have cost nearly £400 million. (page 32)

- On some days, bitcoin mining uses as much energy as Poland and generates 37 million tonnes of CO_2 each year. (page 34)

- Among those British adults who gamble online at least once a month, 17% say they are likely to use some form of cryptocurrency in the next 12 months, according to YouGov data. (page 36)

- Nearly one in seven British adults have used bitcoin in the last year. About a quarter have used Etherium (24%) and 18% have used Binance coin. (page 36)

- Sweden is gearing up to become the first cashless nation in the world, with an economy 100 percent digital by 2023. (page 39)

Budget

A financial plan used by governments, businesses or individuals to manage income and expenses.

Bursary

An amount of money given to a student by the college or university they attend. It does not have to be paid back.

Credit card

A card that is issued, usually by a bank or business for purchasing goods or services on credit. Credit is essentially a promise to pay for something later – this is then paid back. While the debt remains unpaid, it will continue to increase with interest until it is paid off in full.

Cryptocurrency

A cryptocurrency is a digital or virtual payment system, such as Bitcoin, that doesn't rely on banks to verify transactions.

Debt

Something, usually money, that is owed and needs to be repaid.

GDP

GDP or gross domestic product is a measure of the size and health of an economy.

Household income

The combined amount of money earned by all members of a household.

Inflation

A measure of the rate of rising prices of goods and services in an economy.

Interest

A charge that is added while a debt continues to be owed.

Loan

An amount of money that is borrowed and is expected to be paid back, usually with interest.

Mortgage

A loan taken out to pay for a property which is paid back with interest.

Overdraft

Money that is withdrawn from a bank account and causes the balance to fall below zero.

Pension

When someone reaches retirement age, they are entitled to receive a regular pension payment from the government. This payment takes the place of a salary. Many people choose to pay into a private pension fund throughout their career, in order to save extra money for when they retire. Often, employers also pay into a pension fund for their employees. The State Pension Age is gradually increasing. The Pensions Act 2011 will saw the State Pension Age for both men and women increase to 66 in October 2020 to `keep pace with increases in longevity (people living longer).

Quantitive easing (QE)

A method used where central banks, such as the Bank of England, print more money to inject into the economy in times of crisis or recession.

Student loan

A sum of money lent to students by the Government in order to pay for their tuition and maintenance fees. It is paid back gradually once the graduate is earning over £21,000 a year.

Activities

Brainstorming

♦ In small groups discuss what you know about money.

♦ What do banks do?

♦ What is the difference between a debit and a credit card?

♦ Do you think it is important to be taught about money and finances at school'?

Research

♦ Conduct a class survey asking everyone to list their monthly outgoings. Create a graph showing how much they estimate they spend, e.g. on:

- entertainment

- food

- clothes

- toiletries

♦ In pairs search online for recent news stories about bitcoin. What have you learnt about this type of currency? List the pros and cons of using it.

♦ Ask your classmates how much pocket money they receive. Take into account whether they have to do jobs in order to receive it or whether this money is just given to them. How often do they receive pocket money? Is it weekly or monthly? Is there a difference between what the boys and girls in your class receive? Produce an infographic to show your findings

♦ Do some research online about organisations and charities in your area that can help people struggling with debt. How many can you find?

Design

♦ Design your own bitcoin.

♦ Produce a leaflet informing people about debt and its causes, and suggest ways to get help and to deal with the problem.

♦ Choose an article from the book and design your own illustration highlighting its key points.

♦ Design your own bank. It should include all the latest technology for people to use. Make it a bright, fun place to visit.

Oral

♦ Have a class discussion about the latest payment technology available which can be used by shoppers both online and instore.

♦ In pairs go through this topic and discuss the cartoons you come across. Think about what the artists were trying to portray with each illustration.

♦ In small groups discuss the pros and cons of the UK. becoming a cashless society. Who do you think will struggle the most with this change?

♦ In pairs create a presentation encouraging older people to use contactless payments. You should point out the benefits as well as the risks.

Reading/writing

♦ Read the article on page 18: *Is too much money a bad thing?* and draw an illustration that highlights the key points of the article

♦ Imagine you are an Agony Aunt/Uncle writing for a magazine. You have received a letter from a female student who is struggling with debt and thinking of leaving university. Write a reply advising her where to go for help and support.

♦ Write a definition of 'a cashless economy'.

♦ A friend has written to you and asked you about cryptocurrencies and if you think they are a good idea. Write a letter back from either one of these two points of view:

- You do agree with the use of them and explain why

- You do not agree with the use of them and explain why

♦ Write an article about payday loans. Explain how these work and how they can lead to debt. Advise people of any other options they could use instead.

Acknowledgements

The publisher is grateful for permission to reproduce the material in this book. While every care has been taken to trace and acknowledge copyright, the publisher tenders its apology for any accidental infringement or where copyright has proved untraceable. The publisher would be pleased to come to a suitable arrangement in any such case with the rightful owner.

The material reproduced in *ISSUES* books is provided as an educational resource only. The views, opinions and information contained within reprinted material in *ISSUES* books do not necessarily represent those of Independence Educational Publishers and its employees.

Images

Cover image courtesy of iStock. All other images courtesy Freepik.

Icons

Icons on pages 4, 22, 23, 24 & 25 were made by Dinosoftlabs, Freepik, iconixar, KiranShastry, monkik, Pixel perfect, Smashicons and surang from www.flaticon.com.

Illustrations

Simon Kneebone: pages 2, 16, 26 & 37 Angelo Madrid: pages 15, 23 & 29.

Additional acknowledgements

With thanks to the Independence team: Shelley Baldry, Danielle Lobban, Jackie Staines and Jan Sunderland.

Tracy Biram

Cambridge, May 2021